Communication policies in **Sweden**

In this series

Communication policies in **Sweden**

A study carried out by the
Swedish Journalism School
and written by Lars Furhoff, Lennart Jönsson
and Lennart Nilsson

The Unesco Press
Paris 1974

P9 2.   S9 F 8.

Published by the Unesco Press,
7 Place de Fontenoy, 75700 Paris
Printed by S.C. Maison d'Édition, Marcinelle (Belgium)

ISBN 92-3-101183-9
French edition: 92-3-201183-2

Preface

Communication policies are sets of principles and norms established to guide the behaviour of communication systems. They are shaped over time in the context of society's general approach to communication and to the media. Emanating from political ideologies, the social and economic conditions of the country and the values on which they are based, they strive to relate these to the real needs for and the prospective opportunities of communication.

Communication policies exist in every society, though they may sometimes be latent and disjointed, rather than clearly articulated and harmonized. They may be very general, in the nature of desirable goals and principles, or they may be more specific and practically binding. They may exist or be formulated at many levels. They may be incorporated in the constitution or legislation of a country; in over-all national policies, in the guidelines for individual administrations, in professional codes of ethics as well as in the constitutions and operational rules of particular communication institutions.

The publication of this series of studies has been undertaken as part of the programme adopted by the General Conference of Unesco at its sixteenth session, related to the analysis of communication policies as they exist at the different levels—public, institutional, professional—in selected countries. The aim of the series is to present this information in a manner which can be comparable. Thus an attempt has been made to follow, as far as possible, a fairly similar structural pattern and method of approach which was agreed between the national institutions undertaking the work.

This survey of communication policies in Sweden has been carried out by three members of the Swedish Journalism School (Journalisthögskolan) in Stockholm: Lars Furhoff, Lennart Jönsson and Lennart Nilsson. The opinions expressed by the authors do not necessarily reflect the views of Unesco.

Contents

Introduction

This survey of communication policies in Sweden was prepared on behalf of Unesco. Its format adheres to the guidelines that were agreed upon by a working party consisting of representatives from the other countries which are compiling similar reports.

The fact that our survey reflects more the needs of Unesco than the current state of debate and research in Sweden entails not only advantages but also drawbacks. In the course of our work we found great gaps in the Swedish research; this can be a stimulus for us and others to try to fill them. On the other hand, we were often compelled for present purposes to fill them tentatively by reasoning in general terms or by straining research findings with peripheral problems. We hope that this will clearly emerge from the text, and that it will also become apparent where we have been compelled to set out our own experiences and impressions for lack of research studies.

According to the plan, the final chapter—here called 'Society and Concentration of the Mass Media'—was supposed to be shaped individually, with emphasis on subject-matter that each country wanted to throw into strong relief. Hence this chapter very much represents attempts at interpretations and evaluations of the development, from which it follows that the arguments pursued therein will have to be even more the editor's personal responsibility compared with the rest of the exposition.

LARS FURHOFF

1 Goals for communication

The over-all goal for the communication process in Sweden may be said to take many forms, in the sense that the information disseminated must embrace as many subjects as possible, that all schools of thought[1] shall be allowed a hearing, and that the information must approximate the communication situation as closely as possible, that is to say that the sender's needs must be subordinated to those of the receiver.

This goal is accepted ideologically at the three levels of the communication process that will be considered in this report: the *official level*, as represented by the government, Parliament and other public bodies; the *enterprise level*, as represented by firms which are engaged in information; and the *communicator level*.

In addition, and this is true of all levels, a system of communication with many facets, one which permits a free exchange of information and views, is held to be an indispensable element of a democratic policy.

1.1 The official level

According to an earlier concept, official measures in the information sphere should be confined to those which facilitate communication, whereas controls and restrictions were considered reprehensible. More recently, however, official engagement both in a supportive and in a regulatory capacity has come to be accepted *de facto*.

Public bodies have three ways in which to bring influence to bear on the communication process: legislation, financial measures and official information.

The Swedish Government has never formulated any over-all goal for its communication policy. On balance, however, all the measures that have been taken hitherto seem to have facilitated the many-sided communication process referred to above.

1.1.1 *Legislation*

Of fundamental importance for the communication process is the principle

---

1. Undemocratic views may also be expressed, but they are seldom allowed to stand unchallenged.

11

that public documents should be open to public inspection. All documents received by national and local government agencies, or which are drawn up by these agencies, are accessible to one and all, journalist or ordinary citizen, Swede or alien, whether he is affected by the subject-matter or not. Exceptions from this public-access principle are few: military documents, hospital records and the like. But as the government has become increasingly involved in business undertakings in recent years (as owners or through subsidies), the range of documents subject to official secrecy has been extended to many which are not accessible because they contain trade secrets.

Another fundamental principle is the protection of anonymity afforded to those who furnish information to printed publications as well as to radio and television. Apart from certain exceptional cases which have no real significance, public authorities may not inquire into the identity of a person who furnishes the published particulars. This means that the general public (or subordinate civil servants) may present complaints to the mass media without the risk of reprisal or other unpleasantness, and that the mass media can often obtain information that was actually not intended for publication.

The protection of anonymity is closely linked to the system of responsibility which holds for the press and broadcasting media. Obviously an item of information that is published on the basis of a statement from an anonymous spokesman may be criminally defamatory to a private person. Since offences committed in the press and the broadcasting media must also be punishable, recourse has been made to a system of 'assumed responsibility'. For each printed publication and for each broadcast programme there is a publisher who is publicly registered. This person is held accountable for the contents in their entirety, even including signed articles and reports furnished anonymously.

The publisher's responsibility is regulated by special laws in which offences against the freedom of expression are defined. Of particular relevance at present is that slander of persons dead as well as living is a crime. By slander is meant statements which are calculated to expose the slandered person to the contempt of others. Such statements may be reproduced only on condition that they are true (or there are well-founded grounds for believing them to be true) and that it may be considered defensible to reproduce them (for instance on account of their news value). The following were recently struck out of the legislation: pornography, insulting the chief of state of a foreign country, affronts against religious liberty and certain other limitations on freedom of expression.

The legal limits imposed on freedom of expression are the same for printed publications as for broadcasting. But under the terms of a separate agreement with the government, freedom of expression on radio and television is further curtailed on the grounds that Sveriges Radio (the Swedish Broadcasting Corporation) has a monopoly of such broadcasting, whereas in respect of printed publications every Swedish citizen enjoys a statutory right to set up in business as a publisher.

The limitation on Sveriges Radio is mainly embodied in the directive to the effect that its programmes shall be impartial and founded on facts. Naturally, the requirement of impartiality is of cardinal interest: it may be seen as an expression of endeavour to achieve, within the monopolistic frame-work, the diversity that the unrestricted right of establishment is meant to safeguard where printed publications are concerned. At the same time, however, the requirement prohibits Sveriges Radio from favouring certain shades of opinion or from taking a stand of its own on the issues that are discussed. Even so, there is one explicit exception: Sveriges Radio must safeguard the fundamental democratic rights among which are freedom of expression and the principle of free and secret elections.

Compliance with these requirements is supervised by a government-appointed Radio Council, which examines broadcast programmes and pro-nounces judgement upon them. Although the Radio Council cannot mete out any sanctions, it operates on the premise that Sveriges Radio will obey its rulings.

The legislation in this field is so designed that offences against freedom of expression are judged leniently and in accordance with a separate code of procedure. Censorship, i.e. the prior examination of subject-matter by public authorities, is not even permitted in wartime. Conversely, this means that a complete freedom of diffusion exists both for printed publications and broadcasting. Everything may be made public, however gross the offence committed against freedom of expression.[1] The public authorities cannot take any action until after publication occurs.

Private persons as well as public authorities may sue publishers of printed publications or of broadcast programmes before a court of law. But if the suer is a public authority, the case must first be tried by the Minister of Justice. Here, accordingly, there is a means of abstaining from legal action if special circumstances exist. When trying cases of this kind, the court is enjoined to be especially restrictive in its interpretation of the law. No reasoning by analogy is permitted to extend the domain of criminal acts beyond the letter of the law, and even the letter of the law must be restrictively construed. If any party so requests, a jury of laymen will take part in the proceedings. Its task is to decide, without having to state any reasons therefor, whether an offence against freedom of expression has been commited or not. If the jury acquits the defendant, its verdict is final; but if it decides for conviction, the verdict may be reversed by the court.

In point of fact, the legal regulation of freedom of expression is so modest, so restrictive in interpretation and circumstantial in application, that a more flexible, extralegal system has been created in parallel.

Under this legislation, the responsibility for printed publications and broadcast programmes rests with the publisher alone; there follows from this a unilateral right for him to determine the contents of what is printed or broad-cast. It is in this context that the rules on copyright take on a special interest. In addition to financial rules, this legislation protects the author's intellectual property. As the law reads, a publisher who interferes with a text or a pro-

---

1. On the other hand motion pictures to be shown in cinemas are subject to prior censorship in order to prevent scenes of brutalizing violence.

gramme—for instance, with the intention of excluding libellous subject-matter—commits an offence against the author's rights.

The publisher's responsibility embraces the contents as a whole. For printed publications (but not for broadcast programmes) this refers not only to the editorial content but also in principle to paid advertising.

In reality, however, this exclusive responsibility as regards advertising has been modified in recent years. As part of tightened public control over commercial publicity and marketing, certain rules have been adopted for advertising. In this context the contents of a newspaper may be regarded as criminal even if they do not constitute an offence against freedom of expression in the ordinary sense. The sanctions are then normally imposed on the advertiser.

Furthermore, the newspaper firms have pledged themselves to insert editorial advertisements of opinions, even if these conflict with the paper's own policy, without interfering with the advertising text (provided, however, that the contents do not contravene existing legal or extralegal rules).

The instruments of communication are not confined to printed publications and broadcasting. In recent years such activities as demonstrations, meetings and bill-posting have likewise been given more lenient treatment at the hands of the government; to all intents and purposes the freedom allowed by law may now be considered absolute when it comes to organizing public meetings and demonstrations. In the latter case, it is necessary to notify the police in advance and, naturally, any offences against the freedom of expression or other crimes committed in the course of meetings or demonstrations can be tried afterwards by the courts. In such cases the 'safety net' that encompasses printed publications and broadcasting is entirely missing; a normal code of procedure is in force. As regards bill-posting, the only latter-day restriction is one that bars the public display of pornographic pictures. However, the right to put up posters is not free: it is limited in practice by the fact that poster space must be bought from the person who holds the title to the land.

1.1.2 *Financial measures*

Broadcasting is one area of communication where the government has reserved to itself a paramount right of decision in the financial sphere. Sveriges Radio, which is vested with the sole and exclusive broadcasting right, may not broadcast paid advertising. Listeners and viewers pay licence fees into a special fund, and Sveriges Radio receives annual appropriations from this fund as voted by Parliament. This is the corporation's only source of income. In voting the appropriations, Parliament may lay down conditions for Sveriges Radio's financial administration and organizational structure.

Programme policy is determined on the principles set forth by legislation and in the agreement between Sveriges Radio and the government.

The communication process receives support from the State scholarships that are awarded to writers and artists.

More specifically, newspapers and magazines are subsidized by favourable postal rates, in addition to which the newspapers are exempt from value added tax on revenues from subscriptions and single-copy sales (revenues from advertising, on the other hand, have to bear this tax.) In part, too, official advertising in newspapers and periodicals is regarded as a subsidy to the press, but primarily of course as a vehicle for informing citizens about public affairs.

The motion-picture industry was formerly subject to a special levy on box-office receipts. This tax has been abolished and superseded by a charge payable to the Film Institute, which among other things awards prizes for quality films.

Financially ailing newspapers qualify for various kinds of assistance out of public funds. A principle for all such assistance is that no strings may be attached in the form of considerations or conditions imposed on the editing of newspapers or the positions they take on different issues.

Thus, of the various forms of printed communication, it is the newspapers on which the government appears to set greatest store to judge from the subsidies given to financially ailing newspaper firms.

Other forms of communication are given shorter shrift. This is particularly true of advertising, which is subject to a special tax of 6 per cent for insertions in newspapers, and 10 per cent for other kinds of advertising and publicity. The explicit justification for the lower rate for newspapers is the financial difficulties of the firms that publish them.

1.1.3 *Public information*

Government at the national and local level needs to issue certain types of announcements to the general public: vacancies in administrative agencies, information about new laws and regulations, reminders to taxpayers to file their returns, etc. In some cases newspapers and other mass media may be expected to attach sufficient news value to these public messages to insert them as editorial matter. Sometimes this is not so and national and local governments are obliged to buy space in the papers. In the case of Sveriges Radio, the corporation may be requested to broadcast the message but the ultimate decision lies with the corporation.

The government may have wider informational ambitions than those just mentioned. A case in point was the changeover to right-hand traffic in 1967, when treasury funds were spent on a huge campaign comprising brochures, advertisements, posters and a series of broadcast programmes to create an understanding for the reform and teach the citizens a new pattern of traffic behaviour.

This massive effort produced the result intended, but at the same time it brought into full relief the whole complex of problems involved in government information, in particular the dangers inherent in any one-way information process as regards bringing undue influence to bear on the citizens. It seems as though the government is not prepared at present to take a definite stand on the controversial issue of public information in terms of its scope and direction. For the time being small-scale experiments are in progress with an annual budget of 15 million kronor. Disposal of the funds is entrusted to a government-appointed commission.

1.2 The enterprise level

1.2.1 *Mass-media firms*

With the important exception of Sveriges Radio, the Swedish mass-media firms are commercial enterprises and are consequently profit-making. Some firms have a non-profit objective which may be more or less explicit, but the order of priorities as between the two objectives is not always clear. Only when a firm runs at a loss, and this loss is made up by the newspaper's sympathizers, can the non-profit motive be assumed to take priority.

1.2.1.1 *Sveriges Radio*

The objective for Sveriges Radio is linked up with the public-service system which operates in several Western European democracies. Under this system the right to broadcast is vested in one or more public utilities which enjoy substantial autonomy and freedom to act as 'a broadcasting service in the public interest'.

As recently as 1966, Parliament emphasized that the radio and television services should be independent in relation to the government and other interests and that they should be organized so as to permit expression of diversity of opinion in their broadcast programmes. Parliament has also stressed Sveriges Radio's cultural responsibility and its mission of raising the general cultural level.

These general principles are elaborated in the corporation's agreement with the government. Among the stipulations are the following:

Sveriges Radio shall uphold the fundamental democratic values in its programmes.

Sveriges Radio shall disseminate, in suitable form, information on current events and inform about important cultural and social questions, and encourage debate on such issues.

Programmes shall be varied in character and content. They shall satisfy, on a reasonable scale, different interests in respect of religion, music, theatre, art, literature and science.

Programmes shall provide good diversion and entertainment, catering for a variety of different tastes.

The more distinctive interests of minority groups shall also be catered for as far as possible.

Programmes as a whole shall be marked by a reasonable balance between different views and interests.

The rules governing impartiality and objectivity shall be applied having regard to the requirement that extensive freedom of speech and information shall obtain in broadcasting.

1.2.1.2 *Newspapers*
Apart from the main commercial objective mentioned above (section 1.2.1),
the following aims may be said to apply more or less to all newspapers.
To inform readers as their primary source of information about current events
(exceptions: the evening 'tabloid' papers published in Stockholm, Gothenburg and Malmö, which are definitely supplementary papers, as well
as certain papers which come out only on one, two or three days a
week).
To provide advertising.
To foster certain opinions, for the most part essentially in agreement with
the stands taken by a political party.
To offer diversion and entertainment.
The principal difference as compared with the objectives of Sveriges Radio
(section 1.2.1.1) is that the existence of many different newspapers is counted
on to provide the necessary diversity and eclecticism, whereas each individual
newspaper is intended as a homogeneous product.

1.2.1.3 *Magazines and periodicals*
Commercially published magazines and periodicals have no other stated
objective than to attain a satisfactory income by means of information and
entertaining. In view of the ownership patterns, however, it may be assumed
that these publications can hardly represent other than middle-class opinions
on crucial political issues. (But given the contents of such publications, the
political aspect is mainly theoretical.)
    Other periodicals are put out by the trade unions and other organizations
with the clearly declared objective of promoting the views of the owner organization on major issues. This applies also to the weekly published by the
consumers' co-operative movement.

1.2.1.4 *News agencies*
The principal news agency in Sweden is Tidningarnas Telegrambyrån (TT),
which is owned by the newspapers but also serves other subscribers, most
notably Sveriges Radio. Its stated objective is to give an impartial, correct
and speedy service to all subscribers, irrespective of their highly varying
requirements.
    The same objective holds for AP and UPI, the American news agencies
operating in Sweden.
    On the other hand, the political parties have some news agencies of
their own, whose ambitions include the circulation of material that fur-
thers the party interests but which is not given sufficient attention by other
news agencies.

1.2.1.5 *Motion-picture industry*
The motion-picture industry contains no firms which avowedly foster any
political principles. But, by virtue of the government subsidies towards the

production of quality films, some firms have been enabled to include the goal of making high-quality films as part of their commercial objective.

The labour movement runs its own chain of cinemas (Folkets Hus), but its bookings do not differ from those of the privately owned cinemas.

Quality films are shown at some municipal cinemas, by film clubs, etc., as well as through an agency called Film-Centrum, which mainly distributes documentaries and shorts.

1.2.1.6 *Cassettes*

The production of audio-visual cassettes has not yet begun in Sweden, but already two trends are to be discerned in the current discussions and pre-parations. One is to let developments be governed by the same ideology as Sveriges Radio, i.e. the 'public-service ideology', in which case the cassette industry would be put under appropriate public control. The other trend is towards allowing private firms to look after the cassette industry under the same conditions as, say, the commercial publication of magazines and periodicals.

1.2.2 *Other firms*

The information activity conducted by other firms may be external or internal. In both cases the object is to facilitate the firm's operations, partly by dissemin-ating information which is directly useful to the receivers, and partly by providing information which can create an understanding for the firm's business.

The goal for internal information is closely bound up with the question of the right of employees to an insight into and a conduct of the firm's business. At times conscious efforts are made to create internal communication situations, in other words an exchange of information between management and other employees.

External information is sometimes hard to distinguish from the firm's marketing and sales promotion. House organs, plant tours, industrial films and press releases are examples of measures on the borderline between external information and marketing. In principle, however, external information does not primarily aim at increasing sales, though it can put sales efforts on a firmer footing.

1.3 **The communicator level**

To be able to do his job properly, the individual communicator must obviously have a goal which dovetails with that of his public or at least does not contradict the goal of the institution in which he works.

It is also generally accepted that no journalist can be compelled to write against his convictions or to carry out humiliating assignments.

Beyond negative formulations of this kind, no material is available about the personal goals of communicators in their work, either from their organizations or in the form of research findings.[1]

The usual view seems to be that the supply of jobs is so varied that everyone should be enabled to realize his personal ambitions. An alternative view is that the professionalization of the communicator's role implies among other things that his earlier political ambitions at work give way to a purely professional ambition, to render communication effective in relation with the public.

At the moment, however, the public debate in Sweden harbours a number of conflicting and, above all, diffuse opinions on these very issues.

1. The Swedish Journalists' Union (SJF) contends that the mass media must exercise their functions of keeping an eye on public affairs with vigour and fearlessness.

2 Mass-media structure

The structure of Swedish mass media bears great resemblances to those in the other Nordic countries and in some measure to the British structure. That is because the mass media in these countries—and in the United States of America—have evolved in close relationship with one another. Sweden's chief contribution is the special legislation on freedom of the press referred to in section 1.1.1.

2.1 Background

The first Swedish newspapers were started in the seventeenth century. One of the founding motives was to provide the government with a vehicle of propaganda at a time when Sweden was involved in war on the European Continent (Thirty-Years War). The need in this situation was to influence public opinion not only on the home front but also in the war-ravaged countries. However, the newspapers must also be seen in relation to trade and much of the newspaper content of that day was specifically intended to meet the need of merchants for information.

At that time there was no question that the newspapers should enjoy any special rights or act in any independent opinion-moulding capacity. On the contrary, the activity of each paper was meticulously regulated in letters patent issued by the Crown. Pre-publication censorship could also occur.

Freedom of the press prevailed during certain parts of the eighteenth century.

This did not radically affect the newspapers structure. If anything, it was diligently exploited to present views on social and moral issues in pamphlet form. A growing literary orientation also became noticeable in the newspapers' content.

It was during this period that Sweden developed counterparts to the English *Revue*, *Tatler* and *Spectator* (notably *Then Swänska Argus*), with emphasis on moral questions discussed in a literary and entertaining manner in the form of the essay, letter and dialogue.

The 'age of liberty' was superseded by reinstated restraints on freedom of expression. It was not until the 1830s in Sweden that freedom of the press returned, but this time it came to stay (except certain restrictions during the Second World War).

During the 1830s and the decades that followed, the liberal burgher class exposed its displeasure with the Establishment and the burghers demanded emancipation from the financial controls of the old guild society, and this liberty to pursue a trade was attained in 1846 and 1864. Demands were also made that the composition of Parliament be modified and the reform of representation took place in 1866.

The newspapers were involved in the struggle for these and other reforms, first and foremost *Aftonbladet* in Stockholm (founded in 1830). Throughout the 1830s the government tried to interfere with the press through confiscations, but the attempts were sabotaged and the criticism could not be silenced. Furthermore, as noted, before long the newspapers gained their rights: conditions changed in the way they demanded and their sympathizers acquired political power.

The liberal 'opinion newspapers' gradually compelled the older newspapers to take a political stand, and around 1870 the daily press became divided into two political camps—liberal and conservative. At the same time the right of newspapers to express criticism of society was affirmed, as was the formal freedom of the press. From this time on the newspapers were regarded as a very important social factor, as institutions entitled to mould their own 'extra-parliamentary' opinion, as a 'third estate' empowered to pursue its aims without having to pay deference to the two other 'estates'—Parliament and the government.

New political controversies cropped up over tariffs, national defence and suffrage. Of all the interested parties, the newspapers are believed to have had a considerable influence on the outcome of these issues. The consequence was not only a growing political commitment among the newspapers, but papers were also started to look after special interests in different domains. When the present party structure took shape in the years around 1900, new papers sprang up all over the country. In addition to the earlier conservative and liberal newspapers, social democratic papers were now founded, followed later by organs for the centre party and the communists. The number of newspapers reached a peak of about 230 around 1920—as compared with the 100 or so dailies appearing today, fifty years later.

The Industrial Revolution hit Sweden in two waves, first during the 1870s and again in the 1890s. To an ever-increasing extent the old economic system, in which the family served as a joint production/consumption unit, was replaced by a market economy. Consumer-goods industries developed, and the standard of general education improved: the first public elementary school act in Sweden dates from 1842.

This course of events brought about profound changes in the economic situation of the newspapers. For the first time they could now reach a broad readership; at the turn of the century, the ability to read was general among the young and fairly common among the elderly.

At the same time the consumer-goods industries had a great interest in advertising their wares to a broad public, and the over-all economic situation likewise generated advertising needs.

21

At this juncture the 'penny newspaper' appeared in Sweden, first with *Dagens Nyheter* in 1864 and later with *Stockholms-Tidningen* in 1889. The price was kept low (below the costs of production) so as to permit the widest possible circulation. Assuming the achievement of this goal, the advertising rate could be set high enough to make newspaper publishing a paying proposition. Naturally, the penny newspaper also had important consequences for the editorial content. In view of the circulation aimed at the material had to be made more popular and sensational, and this type of material given more space than in the past.

Once the principle of the penny newspaper had gained a footing, all the other dailies gradually adopted it; competition for readers quite ruled out substantially higher prices.

With the introduction of universal suffrage around 1920, the political climate in Sweden became less turbulent. The need of politically differentiated newspapers appears to have diminished, and newspaper development was determined to a growing extent by commercial factors. The trend was towards a concentration of financial power; the normal pattern in Sweden today is a single newspaper in each geographical area.

Although today's higher standard of living has increased the consumption of newspapers, this does not seem to have led to the reading of competitive papers of different political shades. Instead, there has been an increase in supplementary papers from the large cities, with more emphasis on the lighter side than the primary paper. These so-called tabloids appeared in Stockholm in the early 1930s (as the result of a reorganization of *Aftonbladet*) and in the provinces after the Second World War (e.g. *Expressen*, founded in 1944 and now the largest newspaper in Sweden).

The founding of Tidningarnas Telegrambyrån (TT) in 1921 may be seen as an indicator of the calmer political climate. It came into being after the First World War. A period of keen rivalry in the press and among news agencies which had taken different attitudes to the war, ended with the founding of TT.

The 1920s also witnessed the introduction of a new mass medium for Sweden: radio. Regular broadcasts made their debut in 1923. They have always been kept free of commercials and their sole source of revene is the licence fee. The sole and exclusive right to broadcast is vested in Sveriges Radio (formerly called Radiotjänst). This company is owned by the business community, the organized social movements and the press.

At first the press maintained a very strict attitude to the new medium. The general manager of TT was at the same time general manager of Radiotjänst, and the whole news service was handled by TT. The governing philosophy was idealistic: the radio was to be used in the service of popular education in order to enrich the audience, especially with experience of a literary and musical nature.

Radio broke through as a news medium during the Second World War; at the same time newspaper circulations sky-rocketed. After that radio was allowed to build up its own newsgathering network. TT news is still broadcast but Sveriges Radio's own newscasts are much more numerous and more detailed. However, TT provides the basic coverage together with other news agencies.

The post-war period brought another breakthrough for Swedish radio, this time as the purveyor of mass entertainment. Yesterday's idealism gradually gave way to a professional ideology: radio is called upon to satisfy all needs of the public and promote its own development. But in opposition to this is another ideology, especially in the field of public affairs: the group-oriented. Established sections of the community (represented on the board of Sveriges Radio, among others) want the radio service to give a positive picture of Swedish society and to further the interests that the different groups wish to safeguard.

When television made its *début* in 1956, the broadcasts were entrusted to Sveriges Radio. In a word, the same organization and ideology took over as for sound radio. Television caught on very rapidly. The first to feel the blow was sound radio, which had to reorient its operation by going in for light entertainment (non-stop pop), news, 'esoteric' programmes (classical music, public affairs debates) and regional broadcasts. The commercial weekly press was also hit. On the other hand, the tabloids captured a new market as 'programme sheets' or as adjuncts to television, and in this capacity their growth has almost kept pace with that of the new medium.

The commercial weekly press in Sweden has evolved both in line with indigenous traditions and foreign models. Its largest publisher is Åhlén & Åkerlunds Förlag, which accounts for about half the titles and circulation. Next in size is Allers Förlag (with headquarters in Denmark). After the advent of television, developments in this market have moved in two main directions. First, the market for specialized periodicals has grown; and second, a new market has arisen which can be directly related to the rapid spread of television: magazines with material about popular television entertainers, and short-story magazines.

Swedish film-making and the cinemas were hard hit by television. Up till then the film industry had not been given any form of governmental protection. As a periodically flourishing industry a special tax was levied on cinema attendance. Films were censored prior to screening.

The emergence of television, however, touched off a tangibly greater interest in the Swedish film: the government has abstained from the tax, and these revenues were diverted instead to other purposes, in particular the support of Swedish film-making. Prior censorship is still exercised, to be sure, but with substantially curtailed ambitions.

2.2 Current structure and function

Basic statistics on the Swedish mass media are shown in the Appendix. Among the newspapers, the market distribution and specialization are carried to great lengths. The main groups are as follows:

Tabloids. The two Stockholm tabloids, *Aftonbladet* and *Expressen*, have a nation-wide circulation. *Aftonbladet* is mostly read by social democrats; *Expressen* by liberals and conservatives. The two papers complement one another in their reading matter, in particular as regards entertainment. In the eyes of readers and advertisers they may, in certain situations, be equated with some magazines.

Metropolitan newspapers. The morning papers in Stockholm, Gothenburg and Malmö function as local dailies in their publication area, but they also circulate in the surrounding regions. This is most evident in Gothenburg, in the adjoining areas of which the local papers mostly come out only on three days a week. In such a case the metropolitan newspaper becomes a complement, in particular for the presentation of domestic and foreign events.

Provincial newspapers. As a rule the provincial paper is the only one appearing in its place of publication. It is regarded by the reader as his primary and most indispensable source of information providing not only news from the region but from the rest of the country and abroad. The advertising content is determined by the fact that the place of publication is a trade centre for the circulation area (which means that the circulation area is determined in principle by people's buying habits). In some places, two newspapers are published and as a rule there is a substantial difference in circulation, except in three places where the difference is minimal. These smaller papers are all organs of the social democratic party with a readership consisting mainly of party members, so that there is a political motive in addition to the general inducements to read a newspaper.

The market competition among dailies is between the tabloids (the two Stockholm tabloids vie not only with one another but also with the local tabloids issued in Gothenburg and Malmö) and the newspapers at the remaining two-paper localities. In the provinces the tabloids probably compete also with metropolitan morning papers as complementary reading.

To judge from reader behaviour different functions are assigned to the various dailies. Thus, if a social democratic local paper is closed down, its readers will not switch over to, say, *Aftonbladet;* they will elect to read the local paper.

Other printed publications may be divided into the following groups:

General periodicals (magazines). These consist of commercial weeklies and a number of publications issued for other reasons—the consumer co-operative weekly, trade union papers addressed to the whole family, magazines emanating from the private distributing trade (the ICA food chain, for example). In principle, all these publications circulate throughout Sweden. The market is divided up mainly along social lines, with separate magazines for women, men, families, etc. The general periodicals are not primarily read for information purposes; their most special functions are to offer relaxation and to give practical advice and tips.

Special periodicals. The publications in this group concentrate on particular spheres of interest (economics, boats, food, etc.). Newspapers, general periodicals, radio and television usually deal with the same spheres, but more superficially. Those who want more exhaustive information can obtain it from the special periodical.

Trade journals. Many of these are owned by interested organizations, but there are also examples of commercial publication. Their contents are concentrated on subject-matter which is of special interest to an occupation or an industry. From the viewpoint of advertisers, the trade journals are closely related to the direct-mail form of advertising. Normally, the trade journals depend very much on advertising revenues, which may account for as much as 90 per cent of their income from all sources.

Ad. sheets. These papers are distributed free of charge and are completely financed out of advertising revenue. The basis for publication may be either local advertising needs or needs allied to advertising in special periodicals.

The role of radio as a mass medium has already been considered in section 2.1. Generally speaking, newscasts command a high degree of listener appeal, as do regional broadcasts.

Television has come to play a major role as a supplier of news, even though the local newspaper must still be regarded as the primary source of information.[1] In addition, of course, television offers a varied output, within the limits of the transmission time of forty hours per week allotted to each of the two television channels. The highest viewer figures are for different kinds of entertainment, including feature films, and sports events.

Research up to the present time appears to lend support to the hypothesis that the mass media perform an information function for the public and that this can be divided into three subfunctions: (a) the didactic or pedagogical function of informing the listening public about current events and their background; (b) the instrumental function of providing for the use of mass media information at work or in leisure hours; (c) the social function, facilitated through partaking of the mass-media content (provides topics of conversation, etc.).

The mass media also help to mould opinion, usually in the sense that media contents may pre-establish attitudes among the public. Only in exceptional cases (for instance, the changeover to right-hand traffic) can it be assumed that the mass media have led to changing public attitudes.

The mass media obviously have an entertainment function too.

In recent years increasingly greater weight has been attached to the ritual function of the mass media; in other words, reading newspapers, watching television and listening to the radio form integral parts of a habit pattern. If the habit is broken (for example by a newspaper strike) feelings of insecurity result.

All these investigations have taken as their point of departure the isolated individual, even though there are good reasons to assume that to a great extent the mass-media consumption amounts to group behaviour. Furthermore,

---

1. The 1967 Commission of Inquiry into the Press reports a study which 'suggests that television is taking over the functions that were formerly fulfilled by radio but hardly—and at least not to the same extent—the functions that were earlier fulfilled by newspapers'.

the research methodology employed lends some credibility to the suspicion that the responses are influenced by prestige considerations.

Therefore, in a very few years' time the research position will probably be very different. We should then have much more reliable and realistic theories about the functions of mass media in relation to the audience and about their potential for bringing about changes in society.

3 Government and communication

A survey of national policy in the information sphere is given in section 1.1 The present section is intended to amplify this survey.

3.1 Newspapers

All newspapers enjoy certain special financial benefits: they are exempted from value-added tax (now at 17.65 per cent for other commodities) on their receipts from subscriptions and single-copy sales; they are given favourable postal rates (according to Post Office calculations, the annual subvention (1971) amounts to 30 million kronor). Further, advertisements in newspapers are taxed at 6 per cent whereas other advertising and publicity are taxed at 10 per cent.

In addition, special benefits accrue to financially weaker newspapers, the 'second-ranking' papers (i.e. dailies with a larger competitor in their place of publication).

Each year (for the period 1969–75) these newspapers may borrow 25 million kronor from the Press Loan Fund. Loans are granted only for measures that cannot be financed by the general credit market at reasonable terms. Very little is required in the way of security. Exemption from interest and amortization is allowed for periods ranging from three to five years. The longest loan period is twenty years. The interest rate is lower than any comparable rate on the market. Loans may be granted not only for investments in buildings and machinery, but also for other purposes (e.g. market adaptation and marketing) which are deemed necessary to ensure the firm's continuity. The loan fund is administered by a board of three persons appointed by the government.

Over and above these borrowing facilities, the second-ranking papers qualify for an annual production grant. The aggregate amount for this purpose is estimated at 67 million kronor (1972). It is payable at a rate of 5,000 kronor per ton of newsprint used for editorial matter. The grant is maximized at 8 million kronor for metropolitan newspapers and 2.5 million kronor for provincial papers. Publications resembling dailies but which are issued only once a week receive a flat grant of 200,000 kronor.

To ease the plight of second-ranking newspapers and render the distribution of papers more efficient, a joint distribution discount has been available since 1970. It is estimated (1972) to cost 20 million kronor per annum. Under this system, which is voluntary, discounts are allowed to all newspapers which turn over the distribution work to a separate company. This company must distribute all papers that wish to participate and charges them the same cost per distributed copy. The effect is to eliminate the advantages of large-scale operation for the first-ranking newspapers in respect of the expensive process of distribution. A primary object of the discount is to compensate these latter papers for the added expense which this entails.

3.2 Magazines and periodicals

Magazines and periodicals also get preferential treatment as regards postal rates; according to Post Office calculations, the annual subvention for these publications comes to 30 million kronor. On the other hand, magazines and periodicals are not eligible for the joint distribution discount, nor may they borrow from the Press Loan Fund, or receive production grants.

Unlike newspapers, value-added tax (at 17.65 per cent) is imposed on magazines and newspapers, including receipts from subscriptions and single-copy sales. Certain association and membership periodicals are exempted. Advertisements in magazines and periodicals are taxed at 10 per cent. But since advertising revenues under 3 million kronor are exempt from tax, the smaller publications actually do not have to pay this tax.

3.2.1 *Financial assistance to periodicals*

Cultural and non-profit-making periodicals receive annual subsidies totalling 1.24 million kronor (1971/72).

Of this amount 200,000 kronor is spent on supporting purchases. The Committee for Assistance to Periodicals (a government-appointed body) sets up a list of a hundred or so periodicals, from which designated libraries may make a selection within allotted financial limits. It is especially stipulated that the list shall offer an all-round selection.

A basic grant of 800,000 kronor was awarded to cultural periodicals. The committee distributes funds as needed towards fostering high quality and diversity.

Lastly, 240,000 kronor in project grants was awarded to cultural and non-profit-making periodicals as a contribution to more expensive projects.

3.3 Broadcasting media

As mentioned earlier (section 1.1.1 and elsewhere), Sveriges Radio is vested with the sole and exclusive right to broadcast radio and television programmes. The State also controls the corporation finances through the annual parliamentary appropriations voted out of licence revenues.

However, the monopoly is conferred only for the transmission of programmes, not for their production. In addition to Sveriges Radio there are a few private producers of (usually filmed) television programmes, as well as a government body, the Committee for Radio and Television in Education (TRU), whose duties include the production of radio and television programmes. These programmes, intended for the education of young people or adults, are broadcast on Sveriges Radio's different channels by agreement with the corporation. TRU's activities are financed out of taxes and payments from individual clients.

The government influence on Sveriges Radio and TRU takes a variety of forms and will be further described below.

3.3.1 *Sveriges Radio*

By virtue of the Radio Act the government in the agreement referred to earlier (1.2.1.1) has conveyed to Sveriges Radio the sole and exclusive right to broadcast radio and television programmes to the general public. The obligations of Sveriges Radio are set out in the Radio Act and in the agreement, as well as in the Radio Liability Act. All these regulations together with the annual financial examination that takes place in Parliament, provide the general framework for broadcasting. If Sveriges Radio violates any of the legal rules it is liable to punitive sanctions, in some cases through indictment before a public court (with competence to try charges of libel), but mostly on the strength of statements made by the Radio Council. Theoretically, the violations may be so gross or extensive that the government, on recommendation of the Radio Council, may terminate the agreement with Sveriges Radio and transfer the sole right to some other undertaking.

Of greater practical importance, however, is that the government appoints the majority of the board of Sveriges Radio, including the chairman.

The remaining board members are appointed by the shareholders: the popular movements, the business community and the press. In its turn the board appoints the officers of the corporation.

Under the agreement with the government, however, the different programme units—sound radio, TV1, TV2, regions, educational programmes—are guaranteed a substantial autonomy.

The board of Sveriges Radio has earlier concerned itself with particular programme questions only in exceptional cases. Its principal duties were to direct financial and administrative operations and to formulate guidelines for programmes. However, these are general guidelines and seldom extend beyond what follows from the legislation, agreements and the practice established by the Radio Council. Of late, however, the board has been paying greater attention to individual programme questions, and there is no formal impediment thereto.

As a rule, however, these matters are left to the decision of the individual division heads, and of late these officers have been exploring ways and means of offering the personnel greater power of decision-making on programme questions.

3.3.2 *TRU*

The activities of TRU are in the charge of a committee of three members appointed by the government. Like other committees, organizationally, it is a part of the civil service, in this instance the Ministry of Education and Cultural Affairs. The programmes produced are commissioned either by national or local educational authorities or by associations. TRU is thus subject to the influence of clients as well as to a direct government influence, extending to particular programme questions. The activities of TRU are run on an experimental basis and at the same time, the educational unit of Sveriges Radio produces programmes having similar aims.

3.4 **Films**

Films to be shown in cinemas have long been subject to prior censorship. It seemed for a time as though censorship would be abolished altogether, the more so since an increasingly liberal practice had been evolving, especially in regard to pornography. However, the censors paid growing attention to brutalizing scenes of violence, and it is primarily to prevent such scenes from being shown that censorship is maintained.

Although the motion-picture industry is not otherwise subject to any specific official control, its financial difficulties have brought up the question of different forms of public support.

In fact, of course, the motion-picture industry already enjoys substantial support from the government. This has been brought about by discontinuing the 10 per cent tax on box-office receipts. These monies are now remitted instead to the Swedish Film Institute. In addition, the institute receives a direct government subsidy of 1.3 million kronor (1972/73).

All members of the board of the institute are appointed by the government. Apart from the board there is an Administrative Council (of thirty to forty persons), which is appointed by the motion-picture industry, the cinema trade unions and other organizations affected by the foundation's activities.

The Administrative Council is called upon to serve the board as an advisory body, to submit comments on the board's annual report to the government, and to designate a jury for deciding what films shall receive quality grants.

Ten per cent of the revenues that flow into the Swedish Film Institute (totalling about 15 million kronor in 1970/71) is set aside for such quality grants to Swedish feature films.

Another 15 per cent of the revenues is earmarked for general production loans and/or production guarantees to provide the making of Swedish feature films. The rules governing this general assistance are laid down by the board of the Swedish Film Institute in consultation with the Association of Swedish Film Producers.

A further 30 per cent is earmarked for the same purpose as above, except that the production loans and/or production guarantees are selective. This portion of the revenues is entrusted to two endowment directorates, each having the use of half the aggregate amount. One directorate is appointed by the motion-picture industry (four members) and the Association of Film Directors (one member). The other is appointed by the motion-picture industry (one member), the Association of Film Directors (two members), the Association of Production and Studio Managers (one member), the section for cameramen within the Swedish Actors' Equity Association, and the Association of Swedish Sound Track Technicians (one member each).

Swedish films produced by the institute itself get 10 per cent of the revenues. Of this amount 70 per cent is to be spent on producing feature films and 30 per cent on shorts.

Five per cent of the revenues goes towards certain purposes common to the motion-picture industry: public relations, film festivals, etc.

The remaining 30 per cent of the revenues is put at the disposal of the board of the Swedish Film Institute for various appropriate purposes, such as: (a) to foster worthwhile Swedish film production; (b) to support artistic and technical training as well as teaching and research on the cinematic art; (c) directly or in partnership with popular education organizations and film studios, to diffuse knowledge of the cinematic art; (d) to contribute to the preservation of films and materials having a historical interest.

3.5 Perspectives

The government has set up a committee to revise the Freedom of the Press Act and the Radio Liability Act. Among other things, the committee is called upon to consider the feasibility of creating a single law on the freedom of expression and its limitations that can be applied to all the mass media. This law, like the Freedom of the Press Act, would have the character of constitutional law (and thus be changeable only by two parliamentary decisions with intermediate elections). Certain less-essential provisions would then be transferred to ordinary law. Parliament has requested the government to set up a new press commission to study the effects of these supporting measures so far established and to propose suitable long-term measures to ensure the continuation of an all-round press.

In June 1972 a new Commission of Inquiry into the Press was formed on which five parliamentary parties and the newspaper industry were represented. According to its terms of reference, 'the Commission should make a general appraisal of developments in different mass media, taking into account technical, economic, marketing and organizational factors. Likewise, consideration should be given to the emergence of new media techniques, such as cable television. The main object for inquiry should be co-operation and rationalization in the newspaper industry, as well as the forms for government assistance to the press'.

Assistance should be designed so as to stimulate co-operation and provide real opportunities for new ventures.

The commission will also consider newspapers and periodicals that are published by non-profit organizations and trade unions. However, its cardinal mission is concerned with the daily press, for which it is enjoined to define specific objectives for State action and to clarify the role of the daily press in relation to other mass media.

The commission is debarred by its terms of reference from inquiring into matters of taxation, postal rates and government information services. Moreover, its proposals should fall within the budget estimates now allocated for press support.

4 The media in operation

The present chapter will be mainly concerned with the institutional framework for media activities, with special reference to factors of the kind that the media themselves can control, either as individual undertakings or collectively. However, this aspect cannot be isolated altogether; consideration must also be given to public measures affecting media operation. Reference must be made, too, to the subject of influence that employees can exercise over the management policies although full treatment of this subject is deferred to Chapter 5.

4.1 Collective measures

As a rule, the measures taken collectively by media firms are limited to newspaper publishers or groups of newspapers. In view of its special status, Sveriges Radio does not usually participate. In principle, these collective measures focus either on concerted efforts towards improving operational conditions or on achieving a stronger united front vis-à-vis adversaries, among which national and local government may also be counted.

4.1.1 Co-operation and organizations

The largest organization in the information sphere in terms of recruitment base is the Publicists' Club, which consists of persons having various links with information: newspaper owners, journalists, authors and communicators. The Publicists' Club administers scholarship funds, lays down codes of conduct (see section 4.1.3) and sponsors debates on publicity matters. But owing to its heterogeneous and random composition, the club has no great significance for co-operation within the mass media. It may be regarded rather as a social club.

The co-operation is otherwise most pervasive in the daily and weekly press. Serving the trade and association press is the Association of the Swedish Trade Press whose principal duties are to look after the interests of member publications vis-à-vis the State, to represent the group in negotiations on postal rates, and to promote a united front in relation to advertisers.

The central trade association for the daily and weekly press is the Swedish Newspaper Publishers' Association (TU). This organization covers virtually all dailies and commercial weeklies. It represents its members in relation to the State, negotiates on postal rates, works for a united front vis-à-vis advertisers and mediates bulk purchases of newsprint for the dailies. In the latter instance the publishers act as a buying cartel vis-à-vis the selling cartel of the paper mills. The price arrived at in the negotiations carries equal force for all newspapers irrespective of the quantity used.

TU has formed a subsidiary that enables its member firms to participate in the joint development of computer technology for various purposes. Although the two biggest interests in this context (*Dagens Nyheter-Expressen* and *Aftonbladet*) are not associated with this company, this collective venture will nevertheless become important, in particular for smaller firms which can benefit from the combined experiences of their larger colleagues.

Operating in parallel with TU are various organizations dealing with the interests of special press groups.

A-pressens Förlags AB owns shares in all social democratic newspapers except *Aftonbladet*. This company is mainly concerned with rendering financial aid to these newspapers, by means of loans and direct grants that are drawn from funds held by the trade unions and the social democratic party. It has also initiated a combination advertising system which offers a substantial discount for advertisements inserted in all *A-press* papers. Working together with this company is the *A-press* Editorial Service, which puts editorial matter at the disposal of member papers, in particular feature articles of nation-wide coverage.

Centerpressens förlagsförening performs similar functions for newspapers representing the centre party.

Förenade Landsortstidningar (FLT) is an association of financially strong provincial papers in the liberal and conservative camp. Joint advertising has also been arranged for this group, though it is not as extensive as for the *A-press*. FLT furnishes its members with a great many articles with emphasis on general feature articles and light reading.

Föreningen Liberal Press and its affiliated editorial service, *Folkpress*, have a more limited scope. *Folkpress* mostly distributes circular editorials and circular clippings and some political articles.

Föreningen Svensk Provinspress represents the small provincial newspapers, above all by trying to encourage their wider use for advertising, but also on other matters, such as postal rates.

Svenska Nyhetsbyrån covers the conservative papers published in the provinces. Its editorial service is fairly extensive and includes both political and general material. The latter is also distributed to some newspapers which represent other non-socialist parties.

Vectu (the weekly press section of TU) serves the magazine publishers above all by building up advertising volume for the weekly press, for instance by undertaking large-scale collective analyses of readership for the various magazines.

In addition to TU and these group organizations, there are a number of services agencies common to the daily and weekly press. No doubt the most important of these is *Tidningarnas Telegrambyrån* (TT), the joint news agency that is treated at greater length in section 4.4.1.

In large part, too, the distribution of newspapers is handled collectively. All single copies and a large part of subscriptions are distributed by *Svenska Pressbyrån*, which is owned by newspaper and magazine publishers. The remaining subscriptions are handled by the Post Office (magazines, periodicals and certain newspapers) or by privately owned newspaper firms. Such distribution, however, has become less common since the introduction by the government of the joint distribution discount (see section 3.1).

The circulation of dailies and weeklies is audited by *AB Tidningsstatistik*, which is owned by the newspaper publishers (through TU), the advertisers and the advertising agencies.

Together with other interested parties TU also supports a number of institutions concerned with research and education: the Press Institute (refresher courses for journalists), the Graphic Institute (for the training of printing foremen), the College of Communication and Advertising, the Newspapers' Training Council, the Newspapers' Technical Council, the Graphic Research Laboratory, the Swedish Press Archives and the Press Museum Association. TU is also a principal of the Press Fair Practices Commission (see section 4.1.3).

To sum up, this apparently impenetrable forest of liaison and co-operative bodies is witness to the united front forged by the daily and weekly press in the following important areas:

1. Vis-à-vis the State on financial and legal matters, where TU is the co-ordinator.
2. Vis-à-vis the paper mills, here again with TU as co-ordinator.
3. Vis-à-vis the Post Office, but here the interests of different newspapers and magazines are sometimes in conflict and therefore TU obviously cannot present a solid front.
4. Vis-à-vis the advertisers, where TU upholds the principle of standard prices as against different groups which seek to promote their own advertising programmes.
5. In regard to technical research, consultation and training.
6. In regard to the training of journalists, although the media associations have amplified the central efforts of the Press Institute.
7. In regard to editorial co-operation, in which the different group organizations sometimes play a major role.
8. In regard to the distribution of single as well as subscribed copies.

This broad co-operation does not altogether restrain competition between the firms but causes it to be concentrated in fields falling outside the area of co-operation. Since much of this co-operation amounts to protecting the firms' revenues and cutting their expenditures in certain fields, competition has become mostly a matter of cost competition. In other words, the financially healthy firms have been able to narrow the market for the ailing firms by raising the level of aspiration, for instance in regard to editorial content.

In important spheres the co-operation has been extended across party lines. This means that the State and other adversaries have found it hard to assert themselves against the press, the information about current events including such events as the actions against adversaries taken by the press itself.

4.1.2 *Restraints on competition*

As already mentioned, TU stands for the principle of fixed prices and fixed discounts, thus ruling out competition in the form of granting discounts higher than the official rates.

For a long time newspapers in the same locality have usually charged identical subscription and advertising rates, and changes of prices are regularly made by a large number of papers at the same time. Only in exceptional cases has it been possible to prove that such action has been preceded by formal agreements between firms (which is prohibited by law).

Be that as it may, there is no denying that price competition in the traditional sense does not exist in the newspaper industry.

The State joint distribution discount is an attempt to eliminate cost competition between newspapers in the distribution sector. According to proposals made in public debate, the government should also try to check cost competition in other respects, so as to lessen the economic advantages enjoyed by the well-off newspapers and, if possible, afford greater scope for competition in terms of content and quality.

4.1.3 *Ethical rules and internal sanctions*

As noted in section 1.1, there is very little government regulation of freedom of expression. From time to time, therefore, questions have arisen as to whether the legislation should not be made more stringent, above all in order to protect individuals against undeserved suffering. The reaction to such proposals, especially among the press organizations, has been an intensification of efforts to tighten up the extralegal system of internal self-regulation.

One indicator of this self-policing policy is the set of publishing rules framed by the Swedish Publicists' Club; these were first adopted in 1923 and most recently revised in 1970. Compliance with them is called for not only from all newspaper firms but also from radio and television. However, the rules are no more than a code of conduct; they are not directly linked to any system of sanctions. Even so, they can influence the judgements made by the Radio Council and the Press Fair Practices Commission (about which more below).

The stated aims of the publishing rules are to guard against the spread of messages that are incorrect or that can do harm because they are incomplete, and to protect the individual against undeserved suffering. In addition to requiring objectivity and impartiality, the rules also attempt to specify different kinds of undesirable publicity.

Emphasis is put on rules to protect the individual, especially in connexion with coverage of crimes. The main headings are: 'judge no one unheard', 'respect privacy', 'be careful with names', 'show consideration', 'be careful with pictures' and 'allow an opportunity for rebuttal'.

36

The Press Fair Practices Commission has been acting as a court of honour for publicity matters since 1916. Its sponsors are the Publicists' Club, the Newspaper Publishers' Association and the Swedish Journalists' Union.

The commission consists of three members appointed by the sponsor organizations, plus two members unconnected with the press to represent a consensus of opinion. These two members are appointed by one of the parliamentary Ombudsmen (commissioners) together with the chairman of the Swedish Bar Association. The five members appoint the chairman of the commission, traditionally a justice or former justice of the Supreme Court. The chairman has the casting vote.

Anyone may lodge a complaint with the commission; the complainant need not himself be affected by the message or consider himself wronged as is the case for example in press libel suits. Another difference compared with what is punishable by law is that not only private persons but also companies, societies and other associations ('juridical persons') may lodge a complaint with the commission. Since these legal bodies enjoy no legislative protection, the commission is their only chance to protest against what they hold to be transgressions in the press.

A verdict by the commission usually takes the form of a statement of acquittal or conviction of the defendant newspaper. A conviction may be worded more or less sharply. If the offence is considered serious, the commission orders the paper to pay a 'service charge'; this is a sort of fine that goes towards the commission's operating expenses.

A hearing before the commission does not debar the case from being tried also by a court of law. However, a statement by the commission offers no immediate guidance as to how a court would judge; that is because the commission convicts in many cases which are not in themselves a violation of the law. Of guiding—but not binding—force for the commission's judgements are the aforementioned publishing rules of the Publicists' Club and earlier statements of the commission.

Working alongside the Press Fair Practices Commission is the Press Ombudsman. The latter is appointed by a body consisting of one of the parliamentary commissioners and the chairmen of the Swedish Bar Association and of the Press Co-operation Council (a joint body for the Swedish Publicists' Club, the Swedish Newspaper Publishers' Association and the Swedish Journalists' Union).

The primary task of the Press Ombudsman is to examine complaints lodged with the Press Fair Practices Commission. If he finds them to be justified, he must personally request a public statement from the commission about the incriminated newspaper account. (If the Ombudsman finds the complaint unjustified, the complainant may himself take the case before the commission.)

In addition, the Press Ombudsman is vested with a right of initiative. That is to say, he may himself complain to the commission of what he holds to be an infraction of good publicity ethics. In consultation with a complainant he may also help to reach an amicable settlement with the newspaper, for instance by having the paper publish a rebuttal or by himself rectifying a misrepresentation.

The office of the Press Ombudsman was established in 1969, at a time when the Press Fair Practices Commission was expanding and the press was waging a campaign in favour of setting its own house in order. This campaign can be partially traced to the proposals for tightened government supervision of press ethics, which were being discussed in Parliament, but which were rejected on grounds that the press was doing its own house-cleaning.

However, the commitment to self-policing in lieu of more stringent legislation is not unchallenged. According to the advocates of the former policy, the effects of a harsher law would be to curtail the freedom of the press. The opposing camp argues that a quasi-judicial system should be avoided in as many sectors of society as possible; not only that, but the sanctions imposed by the Press Fair Practices Commission are not so rigorous as they would be under judicial procedure, and thus lack the necessary deterrent effect.

4.1.4 *Industrial relations*

As yet it has been possible to broaden the consensus reached by the press on self-policing and various other activities so as to include the sphere of industrial relations. Two employer organizations are still active, one for the social democratic press outside Stockholm, the other for all other newspapers and magazines. Except for one clause, identically worded collective agreements are applied by both of them—A-pressens Samorganisation and Tidningarnas Arbetsgivareförening. So far, however, all attempts to amalgamate them have failed.

Both the employer organizations have long striven for peaceful industrial relations in the newspaper industry on the basis of so-called peace agreements, i.e. collective agreements running for a period of ten years. No direct action may be resorted to while the agreement is in force; instead, disputes that cannot be resolved by negotiation must be referred to arbitrators for settlement.

The first peace agreement was reached in 1937 between the two employer organizations and three national unions (for typographers, lithographers and bookbinders). This agreement has been successively prolonged and is still in force.

A peace agreement reached in 1969 with the Swedish Journalists' Union explicitly stated that the parties wanted 'to help ensure that no barriers are raised to the free moulding of democratic opinion by direct action within that part of the mass media which the parties represent'. This agreement has come in for criticism within the Journalists' Union. 'We were taken by surprise', said the critics, adding that it is thoughtless of a union to divest itself even of the right to threaten direct action. However, the union leaders who signed the contract were reconfirmed in office by a huge majority.

4.1.5 *Research and education*

As indicated in section 4.1.1, the Swedish Newspaper Publishers' Association is engaged in many research and educational activities.

For practising journalists the Press Institute arranges courses and conferences usually running for two to five days in collaboration with the Swedish Journalists' Union, Sveriges Radio, the Swedish Newspaper Employers' Association and the Joint Organization of Social Democratic Newspapers (the *A-press*). This programme is financed by founder donations, course fees and budget appropriations.

The Newspapers' Educational Council is a joint body for the Swedish Newspaper Publishers' Association, the Swedish Newspaper Employers' Association and the Joint Organization of Social Democratic Newspapers. It organizes courses and conferences for the technical and administrative newspaper personnel.

The same founders stand behind MASSK, a committee for mass media research. Although the committee has no research funds of its own, its staff (including a part-time secretary) seeks to communicate up-to-date research findings to the media people and to stimulate research of importance to the mass-media sector.

Corresponding functions in publishing technology are performed by the Newspapers' Technical Council, which works in co-operation with the counterpart bodies in the other Nordic countries. But unlike MASSK the council possesses its own funds so that it not only furnishes technical advice but also contributes to the financing of research and development projects.

4.2 Measures on the business level

Newspaper and magazine publishing usually aims at turning out a product that can yield a satisfactory return on investment, although the satisfaction of goals that cannot be estimated in terms of money is also taken into consideration. The product must have an identity, some characteristic which distinguishes it from other products on the market. Its fortunes are otherwise primarily determined by the firm's financial management. Normally these factors combine to make for a hierarchic structure of authority and to vest ultimate decision-making in the firm's financial executives.

There are two main exceptions to this pattern: small periodicals working on a non-profit basis and Sveriges Radio. The latter is required by its agreement with the government to offer a protean output; in other words, it must reflect diversity, impartiality and the balance struck between different interests. Paradoxically enough, the organization of Sveriges Radio has become less distinctly hierarchic as a result. Endeavours are also under way in some newspaper and magazine publishing firms to break up the rigorous hierarchy that has so far prevailed, but as yet the changes have been modest.

4.2.1 *Editorial organization*

In both provincial and metropolitan newspapers the handling of news is in the charge of a managing editor. The principal duty of the editor-in-chief is to direct the newspaper's political and/or cultural commentary.

Working under the managing editor are a number of editorial supervisors: assistant editor, night editor, news editor and county news manager. The provincial paper's sports desk is directly subordinate to the managing editor. The metropolitan paper has a dozen such special desks with a more autonomous status, as well as a number of special reporters who work fairly independently of the assistant editor and supervisors of the same standing.

In other words, the organization at the provincial or metropolitan level is not quite linear. General news material is handled within the traditional hierarchical organization, whereas special material falls somewhat outside this structure. Members of the staff dealing with this special material enjoy a freer status than others; they are more or less directly subordinated to the managing editors.

In the firm as a whole, the possibilities of the editorial office are entirely dependent upon the resources made available by the business management. It is customary to regard the organization of newspaper firms as being 'dual', with an editorial department and a business management as equivalent and sometimes antagonistic entities. However, this cannot be altogether realistic. The editorial office, like the production, distribution and other departments, is one of the producing units in the firm. It must be the central financial management that decides what resources are to be allocated to the various departments and which tries to co-ordinate the work of the newspaper so as to achieve the optimal financial result.

The editor-in-chief and the managing director assume a dual function only when a situation arises in which the board is faced with a decision entailing the choice between an ideological and a strictly economic criterion. In such a situation the editor-in-chief will espouse the firm's ideological traditions as a matter of course, while the managing director has to consider the business aspect.

The organization of Sveriges Radio[1] is set out in Figure 1. Since each programme division has the independent use of the funds allotted, to a substantial degree pluralism has been attained, with a large number of decision-making centres on programme matters: TV1, TV2, the news, the eleven regional centres, sound radio, educational broadcasting, and the external service (Radio Sweden). However, all seventeen divisions are subject to the statutory controls contained in the Radio Act and the agreement with the government referred to earlier.

The central management, comprising the board of governors and director-general, may be regarded as the group management in relation to a great many autonomous subsidiaries. At the same time, however, the board and director-general bear the ultimate responsibility for ensuring that Sveriges Radio fulfils its obligations under law and contract, both financially and in regard to the

---

1. During the next few years (up to 1975) the structure of Sveriges Radio will gradually be reshaped in order to lower costs and reduce the staff.

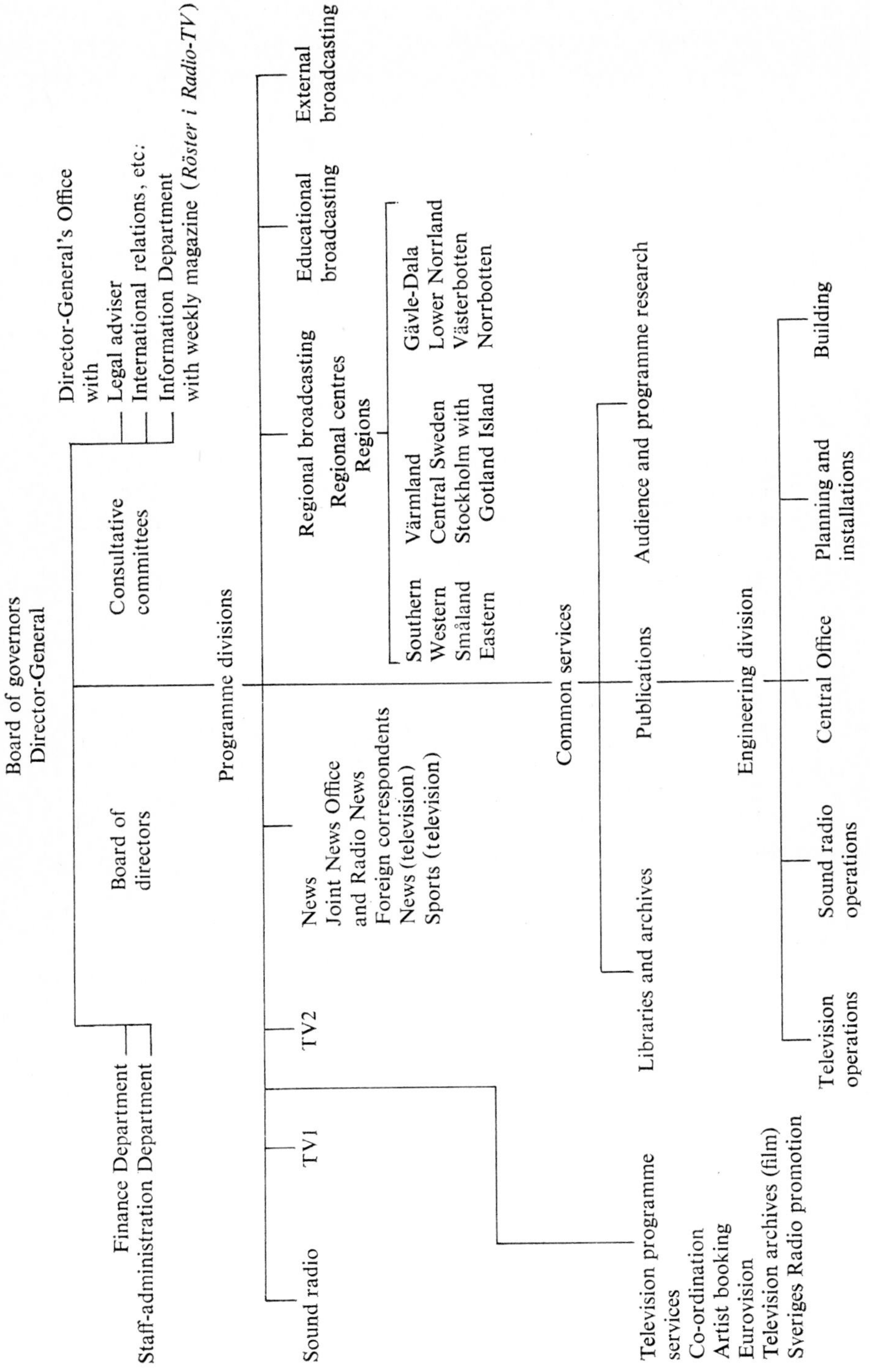

Board of governors
Director-General

Finance Department
Staff-administration Department

Board of
directors

Consultative
committees

Director-General's Office
with
— Legal adviser
— International relations, etc.
— Information Department
   with weekly magazine (*Röster i Radio-TV*)

Programme divisions

Sound radio

TV1

TV2

News
Joint News Office
and Radio News
Foreign correspondents
News (television)
Sports (television)

Regional broadcasting
Regional centres
Regions

Southern
Western
Småland
Eastern

Värmland
Central Sweden
Stockholm with
Gotland Island

Gävle-Dala
Lower Norrland
Västerbotten
Norrbotten

Educational
broadcasting

External
broadcasting

Television programme
services
Co-ordination
Artist booking
Eurovision
Television archives (film)
Sveriges Radio promotion

Common services

Libraries and archives

Publications

Audience and programme research

Engineering division

Television
operations

Sound radio
operations

Central Office

Planning and
installations

Building

FIG. 1. The organization of Sveriges Radio.

programme output. This leads to an evident financial control, but a less marked control of programmes. However, the director-general regularly co-ordinates the political programmes to which the parties are invited during election campaigns. The central management also lays down programme rules which elucidate the provisions of the Radio Act and the agreement with the government. On the other hand, each division draws up its own guidelines for programme policy.

To illustrate how some major divisions of Sveriges Radio have solved their organizational problems, Figures 2 and 3 outline the structure that obtained in 1969 for the two television channels, TV1 and TV2.

TV1 is strictly organized along project lines, which means that all members of the staff are in principle directly accountable to the programme director. For purposes of day-to-day production, however, project groups are formed to deal with individual programmes or programme series. A project leader, who is appointed by the programme director, is in charge of each group. Suggestions for programmes and programme series are submitted by individual members of the staff or outside persons, scrutinized by TV1 and finally evaluated by the programme director in a programme committee (whose functions are advisory only).

TV2 likewise uses a project organization for the actual programme work. The main difference as compared with TV1 is that the members of the staff are assigned from the outset to different programme units and that the planning procedure is formalized with plenary meetings (for policy issues) and work groups for evaluation of programme suggestions.

The organization of the two television channels has become more uniform since 1969. TV1 has adopted the system of project groups, and the plenary meetings seem to have become less important for TV2. One major difference remains, however: members of the TV1 staff move freely between different projects, while members of the TV2 staff are primarily allotted to a number of different 'editorial offices'.

The organization of both television channels came as a reaction to the departmental system that was in force earlier. Such a system—with department heads, section heads and so on—was thought to lead to stagnation in the programme work for two reasons: first, the difficulty of getting through programme suggestions which the department heads disliked; and second, the difficulties of bringing about co-operation across department boundaries. The new structures were welcomed by the staff, especially because they were thought to widen the scope for employee participation and consultative decision-making, and to afford greater opportunities for self-realization and job satisfaction.

4.2.2 *Ownerships*

The ownership interests involved in Sveriges Radio were described in section 3.3.1.

Ownership patterns vary widely for the printed mass media, a state of

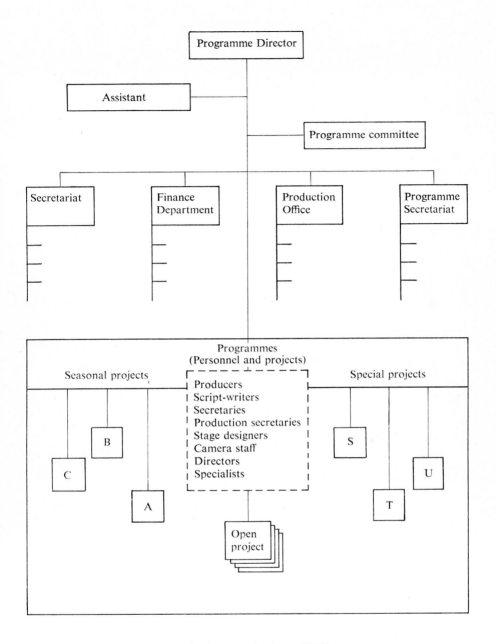

FIG. 2. The organization of TV1.

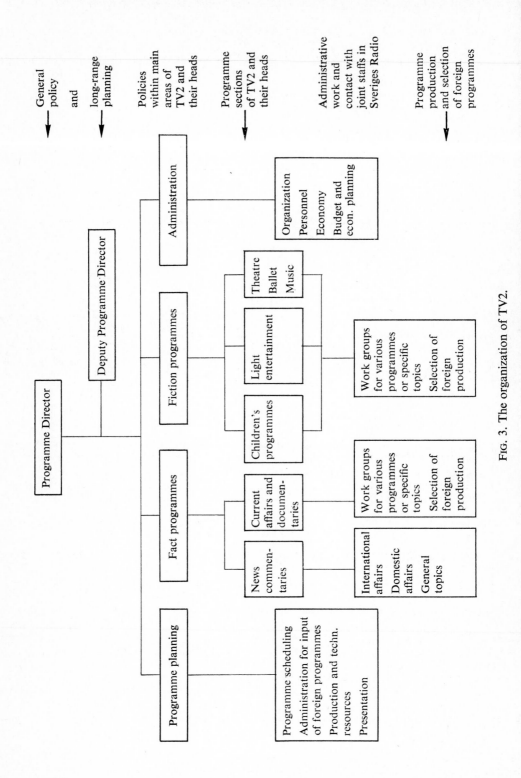

FIG. 3. The organization of TV2.

affairs which reflects the many separate interests represented by the owners. The practice of owners when it comes to intervening in the information process is also highly variable.

Several newspapers and periodicals are owned by interest associations, either outright or via foundations. In these cases owners define a certain ideological compass within which the editorial staff is supposed to operate. This is the case in the newspaper sector for the whole social democratic and centre party press and for a smaller number of liberal and conservative papers. In the periodical sector it holds for *Vi*, the weekly magazine of the co-operative movement, as well as for a number of trade union and association publications.

In these cases the owners' incentives are chiefly idealistic, and their commercial interest in publication is usually not very noticeable. This confers on financially successful publications a high degree of immunity to owner interference; and conversely, for financially ailing firms, a lack of the direct ownership interest which obtains in corresponding situations in private companies, a lack which may result either in drastic shutdowns or stubborn commitment to a declining product.

Private enterprise owns most of the newspapers of the conservative and liberal parties, as well as the big circulation magazines and a number of trade journals. Sometimes the ownership is split up among a number of interests; the shares of one firm (Dagens Nyheter-Expressen) are listed on the stock exchange (but still dominated by one owning family). The general rule, however, is for one owner or an owning family to hold a majority of the capital stock (in the case of Dagens Nyheter-Expressen, this is the Bonnier family, which also owns the largest periodical publishing company—Åhlén & Åkerlund AB—whose range covers magazines, special periodicals and trade journals, as well as the largest book-publishing house).

In some cases representatives of the owners occupy executive positions as managing directors or editors-in-chief. From this it follows that the owners also exercise a substantial influence over the day-to-day work. This pattern holds for many provincial newspapers and for Åhlén & Åkerlund.

In other cases the day-to-day business is completely run by personnel recruited from outside the owning family. Cases in point are *Dagens Nyheter* and *Expressen*. Here the current work—with sporadic exceptions—seems to be entirely left to the staff unless they deviate noticeably from the owner's policy in which case they may be replaced. In special situations, for example when a new paper goes into business or a firm is running at a loss, the direct owner influence will probably be more strongly felt.

4.2.3   *Editorial recruitment*

The educational standards for recruitment of editors vary from one firm to another. Generally speaking, Sveriges Radio appears to attach the greatest importance to educational merits, but there, as in other mass-media firms, professional skill is more highly valued than formal qualifications. The two factors, of course, are not unrelated. Given the high educational level at Sveriges

Radio, a high professional level and a fairly high salary are bound to follow. This presumably stems from the corporation's desire to meet the demands of the State for high quality.

As for recruitment to metropolitan newspapers, their goals are probably virtually the same as regards 'human capital' as those of Sveriges Radio. However, the provincial newspapers generally, and the smaller locals in particular, recruit some people with no experience of journalism and often with a modest general education.

Recruitment to magazines and special periodicals largely follows the same pattern as for the metropolitan papers, whereas the requirements for trade journals and the association press vary considerably.

The firms reserve the right to recruit staff as they see fit, and neither in theory nor in practice do they accord preference to those who have formal training in journalism. Recruitment is based to a high degree on professional achievements acquired in earlier jobs. There is little systematic merit rating and no organized labour exchange.

Employers are bound by collective agreements to consult the trade union in regard to employee dismissals.

4.2.4 *Experiments in corporate democracy*

Newspaper publishers have not been left untouched by the public debate on corporate democracy, which calls for greater employee participation in management.

The debate has so far been rather vague, however, as regards the scope and the forms of consultative decision-making for editorial staff. Newspaper editorial staff has long been held to represent 'intellectual capital', and as such has been granted a unique status. A type-setter is supposed to compose a text whether he likes it or not, while a journalist is debarred by the collective agreement from undertaking humiliating assignments. From this a tendency has evolved to reserve for editorial staff the right to a say on communication contents. The editors would also like to be put on an equal footing with other personnel categories in regard to such other problems as production cutbacks, dismissals and reorganizations.

One of the arguments advanced against giving the editorial staff a voice in the formulation of editorial policy is that the communications situation *per se* implies that it makes no difference what the type-setter or the journalist thinks of a text; it is the interest of the public that must be borne in mind, and that this is a matter which rests with the owner-publisher.

This line of thought is felt to tie in with the conception of the newspaper as a homogeneous product, with a universal image, a consistent editorial policy, the conception of a paper as a 'good friend of the reader'.

However, this philosophy needs to be reviewed in light of the changes that the mass media are undergoing. Sveriges Radio, as the holder of a *de facto* monopoly, must build up its image by offering a many-sided output. Most newspapers have carved out a similar monopoly in their local markets, and there is little tendency to build 'images' for such papers. Actually, the majority are 'community papers', which must pay reasonable attention to all shades of public opinion (in the knowledge that no alternative newspaper exists).

No comparable monopolization is observable in the magazine market but to offset that, the concentration of ownership is pronounced, with 50 per cent of the circulation in the hands of Åhlén & Åkerlund. The markets for special publications, trade journals and other periodicals are highly monopolized.

This affects not only the public. The choice of jobs for journalists is sharply circumscribed compared with the situation twenty years ago.

It is these tendencies as a whole that presumably lie behind the experiments in corporate democracy that have been carried on within the mass media. At Sveriges Radio these experiments have found expression in a less hierarchical organization, in project groups and plenary meetings, as well as in intensified work within the framework of the joint management-employee council. One objection raised against such co-determination is that it conflicts with the 'public service' philosophy, that it threatens the influence which the public can exercise through the government-appointed board of governors and Radio Council. Up to now, however, this criticism does not seem to have slowed down Sveriges Radio's experiments in corporate democracy; here it is interesting to note that a voice in programme planning is given not only to the editorial staff, but also to photographers, cutters and scenographers. Hence some, but not all, technical personnel are included in the experiments.

The situation among newspapers is somewhat different. In some cases journalists' local unions have been reactivated and have managed to bring influence to bear upon appointments and other matters of importance to editorial policy. In other cases the editorial union has obtained the right to representation in the circle of editorials upervisors, the editorial office management.

Such experiments in corporate democracy have so far been reported from only some leading dailies and the largest publisher of weeklies, Åhlén & Åkerlund. The journalists appear to have sought mainly to assert their influence on the appointment of managing-editor posts. Attempts to push through proposals for improvements in the editorial organization have been given second place.

Sometimes the journalists' union have set their sights higher, but the result of their efforts is not yet known.

To sum up, the drive for co-determination in newspaper and magazine publishing seems to be at a more exploratory stage than is the case in broadcasting, although some tangible progress has been made towards exercising significant influence over decisions vital to editorial staff.

4.3 Relations with the public

Sveriges Radio conducts regular surveys of television-viewing and radio-listening in which the public is asked to rate specific programmes. This research has been carried on more or less actively since the 1940s, so that Sveriges Radio has a substantial body of information about audience habits and preferences.

No material of a similar extent is available for printed publications, partly due to the methodological difficulties of measuring the reading of individual newspaper articles. The existing surveys are of very limited value, as instruments for predicting how the public will appreciate a specific content.

All newspapers and the broadcasting media have relations with the public in the form of letters and telephone-calls, but since these contacts presuppose an initiative on the part of the public itself, it is hard to decide how representative are the opinions expressed.

As a general rule, therefore, public reactions to printed publications are inferred from the circulation figures, and to radio and television programmes from the number of viewers/listeners.

4.4 Sources of information

4.4.1 *News agencies and correspondents*

The news agencies are of special importance for those mass media which provide an up-to-the-minute news service, i.e. for newspapers and broadcasting.

As already noted, the main news agency, Tidningarnas Telegrambyrån, is collectively owned by the dailies. For material on the Swedish scene, TT relies on its own coverage plus the coverage maintained by the local newspapers. TT has a 'correspondent' (i.e. a journalist specially assigned to report major events to the news agency) with every daily outside Stockholm. This system does not work without some friction, inasmuch as the papers sometimes prefer to keep a scoop to themselves. TT maintains its own coverage at the head office in Stockholm, and also at its branch offices in Gothenburg, Malmö and Sundsvall.

For material from abroad TT relies on the British news agency Reuter, the French AFP and the West German DPA in the order named. In addition, TT has contracts with other news agencies in Scandinavia, Western Europe and Eastern Europe. TT also has its own correspondents stationed in Moscow, Brussels and Peking (in partnership with FNB, RB and NTB, the national agencies in Finland, Denmark and Norway).

A recently completed study by Hadenius (1971) shows that TT's news evaluation largely matches that of the leading Western agencies (Reuter, AFP), with the focus of interest on Europe and North America and on subject areas such as foreign policy, war, accidents and crime. This news evaluation is reflected by the newspapers and this holds for domestic material; TT's basic evaluation is also used by the subscribers. While the individual newspapers admittedly publish only a fraction of the TT material they receive, they usually take the cables they do publish intact, and the proportions between countries and subject areas largely coincide with TT's evaluation. This is also true of those newspapers which, like Sveriges Radio, have their own correspondents abroad. Evidently the correspondents are primarily used to give their own versions of events that have already been covered by the international news service.

Sveriges Radio has the widest network, with staff correspondents stationed in London (2), Paris, Bonn, Rome, Vienna, Moscow, New York (2), Washington, Singapore and Beirut, plus free-lancers in Rome, Hong Kong, Buenos Aires, Athens and Tel Aviv.

Next on the list comes *Dagens Nyheter*, Sweden's largest morning newspaper. With one exception, other metropolitan dailies also have foreign correspondents.

4.4.2 *Principle of public access*

Thanks to the principle of public access which holds for official documents (referred to in section 1.1.1), a great deal of the domestic news material is easily available from national and local government sources. The newspapers, Sveriges Radio and TT regularly cover the more important news producers in the civil service: ministries, administrative agencies, courts of law and municipal administrations.

4.4.3 *Protection of anonymity*

The principle (referred to in section 1.1.1), whereby the names of those who inform the mass media are withheld, is probably most crucial in the coverage of police news. Preliminary inquiry documents that are drafted at the search stage are generally classified as confidential information, but the police are not enjoined by law to observe secrecy concerning the contents of these documents. As a result the journalists can obtain particulars from the police, but they do not have an unconditional right to information.

4.4.4 *Private sources*

The degree of accessibility to private sources of news varies between different news sources and different information situations. As a rule, there is no difficulty in obtaining news which the informant considers positive, whereas unfavourable news may be difficult to obtain.

This presents special problems for Sveriges Radio, which is duty-bound to provide impartial and objective information. If an important source refuses to release details, the communication of news on a particular issue would be totally frustrated. In practice, therefore, Sveriges Radio has been granted the right in such situations to make the newsworthiness criterion.

4.5 Relations between the media

4.5.1 *Ownership relations*

As already mentioned, the Swedish daily press is a (minority) shareholder in Sveriges Radio. Earlier the newspapers exploited this position to impede the corporation's development (cf. section 2.1). As matters now stand, perhaps the most striking feature of the ownership relation is the fact that TT daily arranges a number of radio news broadcasts, even though Sveriges Radio has a full-fledged news service.

Another type of ownership relation obtains between Åhlén & Åkerlund and the dailies, *Expressen* and *Dagens Nyheter*, through the Bonnier family. In practice *Expressen* competes with the Åhlén & Åkerlund magazines, chiefly for advertising revenues. There is nothing in this case to suggest that the owners are trying to influence developments in a certain direction. An important factor here, of course, is the presence of other rivals both on the magazine market and the tabloid market and it has therefore been deemed wisest to let the two subsidiaries compete with one another as keenly as possible.

The interest shown in exploiting the market for audio-visual cassettes, especially by Åhlén & Åkerlund, makes it likely that a similar owner relation will emerge between magazines and cassettes.

4.5.2 *Special treatment of media*

As noted earlier, the national government's economic policy favours newspapers in relation to magazines through the charging of lower taxes and subsidies. Such special treatment has not actually been solicited by the media themselves (nor do the dailies seriously complain of such treatment being accorded to magazines). It is significant, however, that Sveriges Radio has not been allowed to buy shares in TT, although it is the agency's largest subscriber. The rationale argued for this is that TT wishes to be independent of State interests (the government, of course, appoints the majority of the board of Sveriges Radio). For the past few years, however, the corporation's director-general has been co-opted on the TT board.

4.5.3 *Public criticism*

Television, the subject of daily attention in the newspapers, is the main target for public criticism of the mass media. Generally speaking, the dailies take a critical attitude to Sveriges Radio, not excepting the tabloids which of course base much of their editorial content on television programmes. As a rule the criticism is not general but deals with a particular programme. So far no competing mass medium has ventured to tackle the whole spectrum of Swedish television in relation to programme policy.

Of late the newspapers have come under fire in some critical books and, for some years, television also broadcast regular programmes which, though primarily critical of the newspapers, did not spare itself. The radio service regularly transmits a mass-media magazine with critical content.

It is remarkable that television has endured day-by-day criticism from the newspapers with great patience, whereas the newspapers have reacted badly to television's press criticism. Television's patience is presumably explained by the superficial character of the criticism and the touchiness of the newspapers and by the fact that criticism of the press has never been a tradition.

5 Communicators

Many educational institutes include information as a subject on their curriculum; the most important of these will be briefly described below.

5.1 Education

The schools of journalism in Stockholm and Gothenburg with an annual admission capacity of 240 students give training for information work in a broad sense. There is a basic course of two terms, one term for occupational training and the other for deeper analysis and study. The course provides a general basic education for information jobs in the mass media as well as in administrative agencies, organizations and firms. The subject-matter is grouped around three principal areas: media (their structure and conditions from the legal and economic points of view), sources (their accessibility and credibility) and tools (language and other means of expression).

The course is designed as a vocational training programme, to be augmented with various kinds of specialized knowledge. Thus all students acquire on the whole the same education during the two years of the basic course and specialization is left to individual initiative.

Since in the past decade a great many journalists have been recruited without prior vocational training and with a poor general education, the government has instituted a further training centre at Kalmar as an experiment. There, in-service journalists can attend fourteen-day courses on various parts of the curriculum of the professional schools of journalism.

Admission to the schools of journalism normally requires the completion of upper secondary school (gymnasium). However, other qualifications, such as studies at a folk high school and on-the-job experience, may be accepted also.

5.1.1 YRK course in information technology

Most universities now offer one-term courses in information technology. These do not provide actual vocational training, but give rather a general orientation for a career in information work. They may act either as a stimulus to further studies and later gainful employment in the field, or as a kind of marginal education, or as further training for those who are gainfully employed but who feel the need for more theoretical knowledge.

51

5.1.2   *The Press Institute*

The Press Institute (see section 4.1.5) holds conferences and courses for in-service journalists. Lasting usually for two to five days, they cover subjects such as offset technique, civics, urban and regional planning, and press law.

5.1.3   *The Poppius School of Journalism*

Located in Stockholm, the Poppius School of Journalism runs one-term evening classes in practical journalism for the various kinds of printed publications, in principle as preparation for trainee service on editorial staffs.

5.1.4   *The Graphic Institute*

The Graphic Institute in Stockholm gives training for supervisory positions in the printing and publishing industry. Though most of the students take jobs with printers or the production departments of newspapers, some journalists do enrol at the institute with a view to future work as make-up men and graphic designers.

5.1.5   *The College of Higher Communication and Advertising* (IHR)

The Stockholm College of Higher Communication and Advertising admits students most of whom hold an academic degree. IHR trains them in advertising and marketing, primarily for jobs with advertising agencies and in public relations.

5.1.6   *The Dramatic Institute*

Since 1970 the Dramatic Institute in Stockholm has been training creative talent for work in theatres, films and other mass media.

5.1.7   *Folk high schools*

A number of folk high schools including those at Biskops-Årnö, Skurup and Kalix, have journalist courses or courses which give a general training in mass-media journalism.

5.1.8   *In-service training*

Since the institutions mentioned above provide a general education not linked with any firm in particular, upon entering the job world students need further education known as in-service training dealing with conditions at and requirements of the workplace.

Regular in-service training is given at Sveriges Radio, which runs its own training courses on a large scale, and in a less formal way at other firms.

In-service training was for a long time the only kind of training offered in the information field. Before the schools of journalism were established (in 1959), the only way to qualify was to start out at an editorial office as a probationer, or 'volunteer' as it was called. During the probationary period, in-service training follows the master-journeyman system, whereby the newcomer learns from his elders and from his own mistakes.

This system is still very widely used and, in fact, over half of the new recruits to the daily and weekly press in the past decade began as probationers, i.e. without previous formal vocational training.

5.2 Unions

Actually, there is only one professional body, the Swedish Journalists' Union, but even there affiliation is limited to employees of the press, radio and television working as journalists and, in addition, certain information personnel in agencies of national and local government. However, a great many professionals in information—the 'PR-men'—are excluded from the Journalists' Union.

The union numbers slightly more than 6,000 members, of whom about 1,100 are women. In addition to handling collective bargaining with the Newspaper Employers' Association and the Joint Organization of Social Democratic Newspapers (the *A-press*), the union looks after matters relating to copyright, corporate democracy and education in journalism, both basic and advanced.

Other information professionals are either not organized or they belong to the trade union which organizes the employees at their workplace.

5.3 Vocational roles and vocational ethics

5.3.1 *Rules*

The Swedish Journalists' Union has adopted rules for its members in the exercise of their profession. For all practical purposes these rules should be regarded as a code of conduct; the only sanction envisaged is expulsion from the union, a penalty that has not yet been inflicted.

The rules call upon the members of the mass media to exercise their functions of keeping an eye on public affairs with vigour and fearlessness. Every journalist must assume his share of the responsibility for maintaining sound principles as regards publishing and in that way uphold the good name of the profession.

The rules deal chiefly with a journalist's conduct under the following headings: 'integrity of the journalists', 'editorial advertising', 'humiliating assignments', 'acquisition of material', 'news sources' and 'publishing constraints'.

5.3.2   *Research on journalism as a profession*

To date research on the profession of journalism in Sweden has been confined to members of the Swedish Journalists' Union.

These studies show that the educational attainments of journalists are generally lower than for other intellectual vocations. Less than half the journalists hold the equivalent of a G.C.E. (upper secondary school certificate), and only about 10 per cent hold an academic degree.

There is a great difference in level of education between journalists in the large cities (Stockholm, Gothenburg and Malmö) and those in the provinces. In the large cities two-thirds have at least matriculated, and one-third have pursued academic studies for at least two years. In the provinces only one-third of the journalists have matriculated, and only 6 per cent hold an academic degree.

The advent of the Institute of Journalism in Stockholm in 1959, the State-run institutes in Stockholm and Gothenburg in 1962, and the schools of journalism in Stockholm and Gothenburg in 1967 has supplied the profession with a great many journalists of comparatively high educational attainments. At the same time, there has been considerable recruitment from outside the institutes and schools of journalism. Thus, three groups may be distinguished in the Swedish Journalists' Union:

1. The older journalists, taken on before 1960, as a rule with a low standard of education but whose numbers include university graduates, most of them recruited during the depression years of the 1930s.
2. Graduates of the institutes and schools of journalism, recruited during the 1960s and 1970s, with a good general education and a formal vocational training.
3. Younger journalists, recruited from outside the institutes and schools of journalism during the 1960s and 1970s. These usually have a poor general education, but some of those recruited as specialists hold academic degrees.

As concerns remuneration, the graduates of institutes and schools of journalism do rather well; on an average, their salaries are 15 per cent higher than those for otherwise comparable journalists. From the point of view of career this group also seems to be doing well.

All journalists are very keen on acquiring further education, especially in social studies, not only those who have received formal vocational training, but also those who have acquired their skills through in-service training.

Some of the research done on the working conditions of journalists comes under the heading of 'gatekeeper' studies, which, as the name implies, are concerned with the selection of news. These studies shed little light on Swedish communication policy. Generally, they show that a certain selection takes place in the editorial departments, and that this selection is in accordance with the general criteria for news evaluation of the Swedish, Scandinavian and English-language press.

The other type of research, partly in the form of participant observations, shows that journalists take a critical view of the work of the editorial departments; they would like more clearly formulated work objectives and better supervision.

This research also deals with studies on leavers from the profession. Generally speaking journalism attracts a great many people who are also active in other professions; more than half the older journalists have acquired other job experience. Almost all drop-outs who leave use journalism as a stepping-stone to something higher: they move on to better-paid jobs in allied occupations, to become for example information officers in national and local government or public-relations directors. On the other hand, the less successful are apparently not 'alienated' from the profession; they stick to journalism.

Most of the disaffection that research has been able to reveal has to do with working conditions, opportunities for insight and self-realization or, in other words, management.

This may be due in part to lack of a system of recruitment of editorial departments, of supervisors. Those who regularly get the supervisory jobs are the successful editors, and there is virtually no provision for training in supervision.

5.4 Perspectives

Clearly much greater attention will have to be paid to the education of information professionals in future, and also on developing the skills of those already in service. There are many gaps: in particular, educational gaps in the profession, and an attempt must be made to bridge them.

The working conditions for information personnel need to be reviewed and up-dated in particular as regards supervision and work organization. Here, however, one comes up against the old tradition to the effect that work with news can never be organized, that the job must be tailored to the news flow. But if experience and the findings of research are any guide, this notion has no real foundation. Only exceptionally (two or three days per year) is the news flow such as to warrant taking extraordinary measures. Hence, throughout most of the year it should be feasible to adopt an organization that has been thought through in advance.

6 Communication and the public

As a matter of course, the mass-media contents and other forms of communication are constantly affected by consideration of the public and the goals of business policy. The public too is always able to react positively or negatively to communication, either by taking notice of it or by no longer doing so. The information professionals learn of these reactions through measurements of public behaviour (viewer figures, circulation figures, readership analyses). Since the information professional is normally the person most interested in the communication process, it is possible that he will take into due consideration what he finds out.

State control over information may be seen as another expression of the influence of the public on mass communications, in the sense that the politicians handle such matters with great caution, so that the measures they take will enjoy wide support from public opinion.

However, citizens exist not only as groups who receive and react to information and as voters, they are organized in political parties, trade organizations and associations. They themselves sometimes need to gain a public hearing for their messages. This is the background to the type of influence on the media that will be the concern of the present chapter. The influence may take a positive form for the media, when parties, organizations, firms and other bodies render financial or other assistance to such communication as they consider desirable. Influence may also, of course, take the negative form for the media, when citizens try in various ways to influence the content of communication (the media are exposed to 'pressure').

6.1 Forms of assistance

In addition to government assistance to mass communications, some measure of assistance is forthcoming from parties and organizations, with newspapers as the chief beneficiaries.

The two largest political parties, social democratic and centre parties, as well as the smallest party, communist, subsidize many of their dailies since they usually run at a loss. As of 1971 the total amount of subsidy was estimated at 10 million kronor.

Newspapers also receive financial assistance from the political parties through loans and securities. The parties have set up separate organizations to handle financial assistance to the press.

In the past, the liberal and the conservative parties also sponsored a rather extensive assistance programme. However, this has been largely abandoned because the papers that were losing money went out of business. Owing to the political and economic structure of the daily press, this could take place without reducing the parties shares in newspaper circulation. Other parties, however, have been compelled to keep up their assistance in order to maintain their shares of the circulation.

During the post-war period, the conservatives and liberals have actually been stepping in as owners of newspaper publishing firms that were previously privately owned. The parties, of course, only buy financially sound newspapers, usually so as to prevent them being sold to another party.

The parties also run special news agencies. They support their papers too, by offering free subscriptions, for instance to young families, or financing mass distribution of the paper (hence to non-subscribers as well) during an election campaign.

Organizations of various kinds use similar channels to support newspapers and periodicals. Here the Swedish Confederation of Trade Unions (LO) is in a class by itself, since it accounts for the most significant portion of the labour movement's financial contributions to the social democratic press. Not only that, but LO subsidizes its own periodical. Indeed, this is a recurring feature: trade organizations and others support their publications through direct grants or by including the subscription in the membership fee. As a result a vital financial basis is provided for the trade union press and a large part of the trade press, as well as for periodicals issued by the Swedish Church, nonconformist churches, temperance societies, etc.

Only one of the nonconformist churches, the Pentecostal Movement, publishes a daily paper (*Dagen*). Ever since its inception this publication has had to depend on grants from its sympathizers, either in the form of individual donations or supporting advertisements.

This kind of advertising, incidentally, is a means for the business community to support newspapers and periodicals. By 'supporting advertisements' is understood those which lack a sufficient commercial motivation, and as such are wholly or partially justified by a desire to help out the publication in question with money. It is often hard to draw the line between this category and advertising intended to create goodwill for the advertiser. In some cases, too, the reverse of support arises: firms abstain from advertising in a paper even though obviously justified on commercial grounds. Only exceptionaly has this taken such drastic expression as to admit of proof beyond doubt.

6.1.1 *Owners*

The board of Sveriges Radio is formally empowered to intervene in matters relating to specific broadcast programmes. For the most part, however, the exercise of this power has been limited to laying down general guidelines for programming and to discussing programmes after they have been broadcast. Naturally, this does not preclude any one member of the board from putting forward, privately and confidentially, some definite views of his own about radio and television programmes, nor that the board has in fact concerned itself with especially important programmes, for instance on drug addiction.

The actual influence of the board is difficult to measure. It cannot be ruled out that views on programming expressed by individual members of the board have been accompanied by threats of reprisal; still, no such reprisals have been demonstrable. Thus, even express threats of reprisals lose their effect, since it seems unlikely that they could be implemented.

Basically, the position is quite different as regards the voluminous public information emanating from radio and television (a case in point is the 1967 campaign on the change to right-hand traffic). Programmes of this type have generally been produced outside Sveriges Radio and offered for broadcast. Hence the final decision remained with the corporation, especially so when the programmes were produced by Sveriges Radio from monies obtained from the National Road Safety Office.

The decisive owner influence over printed publications comes into play in the nomination of management staff. Especially where the selection of editors-in-chief is concerned, efforts are made to find a person who espouses the ideological views that the publication is desired to represent. It then becomes the rule to leave all the day-to-day editing to the employed personnel. However, there is ample evidence that the owners have expressed opinions and desires on questions of detail both with and without success. Similarly, there are examples of editors-in-chief who have left a paper after conflict with the owner, but such examples are indeed rare.

The situation is somewhat different where editorial content and marketing are as closely interrelated as in the weekly commercial press. Here owners are more likely to express views on the editorial content and also on personnel changes aimed at bringing out a better selling product. On the other hand, it would appear that political antagonisms seldom enter into the area of controversy; the conflicts have more to do with the professional tools that should be used to further the common cause the owners and the editors they employ share: to safeguard the paper's circulation and continuity.

The forms of assistance are extremely varied. To a greater or lesser extent, they create a relationship of dependence between contributor and publisher; if the latter gets into financial straits, the contributor obviously has a certain leverage for interfering with the content of the publication. Just how far contributors really avail themselves of this possibility and in what ways they do so, is not clear. What is even less clear is the extent to which the publications themselves adapt their contents beforehand to the wishes of a presumptive contributor.

According to the degree of financial dependence, the relations between contributors and publications may be classified roughly as follows: (a) the contributor is at the same time owner and renders assistance in the form of direct grants, loans, securities or other measures (supporting subscriptions, supporting advertisements); (b) the contributor is an organization which renders assistance in the forms mentioned above; naturally, in the absence of any owner relationship the degree of dependency is somewhat less; (c) the contributor or contributors are individuals or firms that provide cash grants or insert supporting advertisements without having any owner interest in the receiving firm (since these contributors normally share no interest in common other than keeping the paper in business, there is less scope for bringing an influence to bear on publication contents than in the previous case).

6.2 **Pressures**

To subject the mass media to pressure is not normally construed as illegitimate. For instance, it is not considered improper for an association to ask Sveriges Radio for coverage in its programmes. On the other hand, it is thought fundamentally reprehensible that pressures should have such a form as to seek to deprive managements of mass-media firms of their (in theory) sovereign right of decision. It may therefore be said that pressure which takes the form of wishes (even if strongly formulated) is acceptable, but not that which in any respect implies threats of sanctions.

There have been very few research studies on pressures to date. For our present purposes, therefore, the problem must be discussed in more general terms, taking different pressure groups as the point of reference.

Turning to the trade union press and the specialized trade press, some editorial staffs have found it hard at times to assert their claims to independence as against the owner. The controversy has revolved around the question as to who is to be recognized as publisher (in the legal sense) of the paper and thus who shall have the ultimate responsibility for the content. The Swedish Journalists' Union insists that the editor-in-chief should also be the legally responsible publisher, but this principle has not been generally recognized.

As regards staff magazines, house organs and similar publications, they are so obviously related to the owner's other activities that the dominant owner influence is not usually challenged. In recent years, however, demands have been made that the editor of the staff magazine should be appointed by the labour management. This should be seen as an effort to give employees a greater voice in decision-making and to turn the staff magazine into a vehicle of communication rather than of one-way information.

6.2.1 *Staff members, employees*

As a rule, there is a strong institutional framework within which individual staff members must carry on their work. This is composed of various elements: public situation, ownership patterns, editorial organization, legal rules and ethics of the profession, the structure of the news-agency system, a common tradition of news evaluation, and various non-codified professional rules. All things considered, the scope left for individual efforts is marginal. Therefore, logically, staff has often concentrated on nomination of the managing editors, a matter in which they have wanted to assert their influence. In some cases the influence has been extended to new recruitment in general.

However, examples are not lacking of collective reaction of the staff against certain publicity or certain publicity campaigns. Even in the absence of an express threat, such an action (to the extent that is succeeds) naturally connotes pressure in the accepted sense. Naturally, too, a line successfully pursued on the question of an editorial appointment is to be regarded as pressure.

6.2.2 *Advertisers*

Firms of all kinds take countless measures to win favourable publicity in the mass media. They issue press releases, invitations to plan tours, trial runs, and opening ceremonies, arrange courses and conferences for journalists—all aimed at encouraging a benevolent attitude among journalists and to get them to write about the company and its products.

It is also worth noting in this context that firms can accompany such offers with promises to advertise provided the paper writes in terms agreeable to them. In so far as a paper yields to this temptation, a case of pressure undoubtedly exists. It is almost impossible to discover to what extent such pressure occurs; that it does occur is indisputable, but it is usually contended to be rare. Equally, a firm which considers it has received unfavourable publicity in a newspaper may threaten to stop advertising in that paper. Two facts are beyond dispute: (a) such threats do occur; and (b) the newspapers do give in to them. What is in dispute is how commonly this happens. It is usually said to be extremely uncommon.

By and large very little of the advertisers' determining influence over the communication contents is exercised through these pressures. It is exercised rather by the fact that no commercial publication is possible without advertising revenue. This means that the mass-media structure (where the printed media are concerned) is characterized essentially by the available advertising markets and that the mass-media content as a whole serves to promote consumption.

6.3 'Safety valves'

Non-established groups cannot bring successful pressure to bear; they do not own any mass media. What, then, can they do if they are dissatisfied with the mass-media content?

To some extent, of course, they can complain to the Radio Council and the Press Fair Practices Commission. This has particular relevance for intellectuals, who can grasp the ins and outs of the formal machinery, though sometimes other groups have been able to turn these facilities to good account (for instance, with the aid of the Press Ombudsman).

In principle, however, other avenues have been chosen for influencing the communication process and, by extension, the public's picture of reality and the political decision-making process. These activities reached considerable dimensions during the 1960s and there is no doubt that significant results have been achieved, at least temporarily: the mass media have broadened their contents and new issues have been introduced into the public debate. But it is not yet known whether these gains will be permanent.

The active groups fall into three classes, as follows:

Ad hoc action groups, formed to deal with issues that are held to be neglected in the public debate, having to do with urban planning and environment, the extradition of aliens, proposals to reorganize university curricula, etc.

Standing action groups. Examples: groups affiliated with the Viet-Namese Liberation Front, consumer groups, residential groups (concerned with the physical environment of neighbourhoods) and minority groups (representing immigrants, handicapped persons, ethnolinguistic communities, religious denominations, etc.).

Organizations, most notably different political left-wing groups, which issue periodicals and pamphlets on a rather substantial scale. Most of these publications are sold from door to door and on the streets by sympathizers and members, and selling is combined with agitation. The subject-matter, often made up entirely of vehement attacks on opponents, is formulated in the organizational terminology—the 'internal' language.

Apart from traditional public assemblies, the principal means used to further group ends are the following:

Demonstrations, either organized or spontaneous. Demonstrations may serve as a method of directing attention on an issue neglected by the mass media or of showing the strength behind opinions that the politicians allege to be receiving negligible support.

Handbills, distributed in connexion with the demonstrations or along main thoroughfares.

Posters, either legally and in order (put up on approved sites and with compensation to the landowner) or illegal.

Newspapers, periodicals, bulletins, often circulated through unconventional channels (e.g. hawking) and produced by easily accessible techniques (typescript, instant lettering, offset) or by more lavish means. The following have a large circulation: *Vietnam-bulletinen, Folket i Bild/Kulturfront, Gnistan* and *Kommentar*. As a rule these publications aim at a broad coverage, but a deliberate exception is *Kommentar* the qualified contents of which are believed to have exercised an influence mainly on the 'moulding' communicators.

Exhibitions, assembly halls, partly with municipal support.

The 'extraparliamentary' activities of these action groups pursued during the 1960s and 1970s have received wide publicity. Attention in the mass media was first directed to the form of these activities, and the message was relegated to the background. Today the messages are also beginning to penetrate the established mass media.

7 Society and concentration of the mass media

Freedom of expression in the mass media is based on two interrelated criteria: first, that citizens shall be enabled, without unreasonable financial sacrifice, to spread information and to express their views, and second, that citizens shall be enabled to choose between messages with different political bias, and therefore that the structure of the mass media shall make provision for a many-sided approach to all.

According to the classical doctrine these demands were satisfied through the competition between a great many newspapers of differing political beliefs. Every school of thought of any importance had the chance to establish its own organ, and the readers had the chance to choose a newspaper which was in accordance with their own beliefs. The classical doctrine also fostered the notion that, by reading newspapers of dissimilar opinions at the same time, readers could obtain a many-sided picture of events; recent investigations of reader behaviour have shown that this was for the most part a romantic dream.

There has never been any question in the Nordic countries of adopting the same approach in regard to radio and television as to the newspapers, i.e. the principles of free right of establishment and free competition. On the contrary, it has been deemed imperative to limit the broadcasting right (in principle to one corporation) and to supervise broadcasting in various ways.

Efforts have been made to modify this supervision of the broadcasting corporations so as to allow them the same freedom to publish as is granted to newspapers, but no easy solution has been found.

The newspapers have been acknowledged as extraparliamentary power factors ever since the 1830s. According to now-classic leading articles written during the heyday of the *London Times* (by J. T. Delane) governments hold *one* mandate from the people: to rule the country with all the tactical and diplomatic calculations that follow from the practice of an accountable state-craft. The newspapers hold *another* mandate from the people: to seek out and lay bare the truth in the interest of their readers, no matter how uncomfortable this truth may be for those in power. It is this philosophy that has engendered the frequent reference to newspapers as the 'third' or 'fourth' estate.

For purposes of broadcasting, a counterpart to the principle of extra-parliamentary rights for the press has been found in the 'public service' ideology. According to this ideology, the basic premise should be the public need of information and entertainment, not the government's need of a propaganda vehicle or the needs of producers to propagate their own beliefs. The yardstick used to determine whether or not the public-service ideology has been respected is the public appreciation of broadcast programmes.

Hence the fundamental idea behind this ideology is more or less identical with that behind the doctrine of press freedom. By partaking of the programmes the public lends its support to an activity which in part runs counter to government interests; in the press sector, readers confer similar legitimacy on the newspapers by reading them. No right to intervene is ascribed to the government; in principle, any abuse of power held by the mass media is held to be an impossibility, for that would deprive the broadcasts of their audience and the newspapers of their readers. But since the audience for broadcast programmes is not considered to enjoy the same range of options compared with the consumption of newspapers, certain special obligations have been imposed on the broadcasting media, for example that the programmes should be impartial and based on facts.

7.1 Reality and the doctrines

Developments in recent decades have rendered the doctrines for both the print and broadcasting media outmoded. This is largely reflected in the newspaper world by efforts to reinstate the reality of which the doctrines speak, whereas, in respect of the broadcasting media, doctrine has been pushed into the background.

Although the concentration process among newspapers has gone very far in Denmark and Sweden, it is also distinctly evident in Finland and Norway. The end result is to leave each geographical submarket with only one local daily plus a few national or regional newspapers. However, the latter publications have a content which differs from those of the suspended locals and do not purport to furnish more than supplementary reading matter, mostly of an entertaining character.

As a result fewer and fewer readers have been able to choose between competing newspapers. To gather day-to-day information at the local level they have been reduced to the sole remaining paper. To make good the deficiency readers have resorted to national or regional papers, but these are essentially fired by other editorial ambitions.

It follows that the remaining newspapers can less and less lay claim to reader support as legitimation of an 'extraparliamentary' function, all the less since the outcome of competition between two papers is known to be essentially determined by economic factors, and not by the appeal that any one editorial policy holds for different readers.

The concentration of financial power in the daily press is of course linked with concentration in the news-agency system.

Furthermore, the broadcasting firms depend on the same news agencies as the newspapers, while they also largely depend on the same local coverage as that provided by the newspapers. Patently the principle of many-sided information meets formidable complications when it is confronted with present-day reality.

Another factor must be mentioned: parliamentary control of the broadcasting media is apparently becoming more obtrusive. This is most clearly evident in Finland, where great strides were taken towards the formulation of a doctrine of independence for broadcasting as a public service, although considerable parliamentary opposition was encountered. Increased pressure on broadcasters is also noticeable in other Nordic countries.

However, the trend is not exclusively towards greater concentration and control. In recent years periodicals of various kinds have sharply increased in number and circulation. Most of the newcomers are special periodicals and political periodicals, as well as publications addressed to defined target groups. The result has been to add a more universal flavour to information in the sense that the already interested (and this includes the editorial staffs of the widely diffused mass media) have been given new information channels. However, this tendency has received only scant attention in the public debate. This appears to be due to the specially important role of the larger mass media, since they may be assumed to give the average citizen a tool for informing himself on developments and of evaluating events.

7.2 Assistance to the press

Financial assistance designed to prevent further closures has been the principal method of countering financial concentration in the Nordic publishing world. Nowhere has this ambition extended to helping new papers come into existence.

The doctrine of press freedom was long thought to admit only of 'omnibus' assistance, i.e. the same to all beneficiaries. However, closer analyses of these 'omnibus' measures have revealed that they inevitably have varying effects for different types of publications. For instance, if the postal charges in Sweden are subsidized at the same rate for all newspapers, morning papers will be favoured in preference to evening papers, subscription to papers in preference to single-copy sales, and big papers in preference to small ones.

The findings of press commissions in Denmark, Finland, Norway and Sweden have provided a body of research data which show not only that all conceivable measures of assistance to the press have structural effects, but also what structural effects each specific measure would have. At the same time, the press commissions have clearly explained which newspapers are in acute need of assistance to be able to survive.

The recommendations of these commissions have been acted upon to initiate or maintain a number of concrete assistance measures. Table 1 sets out the main features of assistance policy in the four Nordic countries.

It will be seen that all these countries have forms of 'omnibus' assistance —low scales of charges, tax reliefs—which mean least in money to financially ailing firms. But to abolish them would have a disastrous effect on these very firms; they would be deprived of amounts that they cannot conceivably acquire

TABLE 1. Government assistance to the Nordic press (main features)

	Finland (million markka)	Denmark (million kroner)	Norway (million kroner)	Sweden (million kronor)
'Omnibus' measures				
Low postal rates (amounts under discussion)	Yes	Yes	Yes(?)	Yes
Telex rates, discounts	1	—	0.75	—
Exemption from value-added tax on net paid circulation (amounts hard to calculate)	—	Yes	—	Yes
Government advertising	—	—	9	15
Other measures				
Loan funds (government expenditure)	—	2	10	25
Production grants—newsprint subsidies	—	—	7	67
Joint distribution discount	—	—	—	20

by other means. Although this fact no doubt explains why these 'omnibus' assistance measures have been retained, it should not be forgotten that the financially thriving firms have vigorously defended the favours from which they benefit most, and that these newspapers (together with the ailing ones) constitute a powerful political pressure group.

Over and above these 'omnibus' forms, the national governments of Norway and Sweden render special assistance to the financially ailing firms. Sweden has gone farthest, and government assistance there embraces the following measures:

1. A Press Loan Fund, administered by a government-appointed board, which advances loans towards investments in buildings and machinery and also towards measures for market adaptation and marketing, though only to firms that cannot obtain capital on the ordinary loan market.
2. A production grant, so devised that it goes only to the financially ailing firms and which is differentiated to allow for their varying needs (differentiation between provincial and metropolitan newspapers and according to the volume of reading matter).
3. A joint distribution discount, payable to all subscribed newspapers but so devised as to considerably lower distribution costs for the financially ailing firms (whereas other firms, in principle, retain their earlier cost level).

These measures cost about 110 million kronor per annum in the aggregate. Their effect has been to prevent closures of newspapers in recent years. On the other hand, it has not been possible to set up new ventures, nor does it seem to have been possible for any of the financially ailing newspapers to gain ground at the expense of competing firms.

Given this background (and in light of the criticism concerning the production grant), the government has now appointed a third commission of inquiry into the press, in particular to explore the feasibility of improving efficiency through co-operation between newspaper publishing firms.

Bearing in mind experience to date, it may be asked whether it is at all possible for the body politic to preserve today's press structure in the long run by granting economic assistance.

No proposals have been put forth in the Swedish debate for forms of assistance that are entirely new in concept (although the amount of the production grant was more than doubled as recently as 1972). An idea that has emerged from time to time is to put greater restraints on competition, for instance, by maximizing the permissible volume of reading matter or by control of advertisement rates (with a view to keeping them down in the case of financially strong firms). However, these proposals are deemed to be politically impracticable, and it may also be doubted whether they could radically change the situation.

Over and above the assistance measures, Sweden has introduced a space advertising tax; in terms of kronor, of course, this hits the largest firms harder than the smaller ones. The end result, however, seems to have been to cut down advertising in the second-ranking papers more than would otherwise have been the case. So far as can now be judged, this tax has aggravated the position of the financially ailing firms—at the same time it has made room in government budgeting for increased press assistance.

7.3 Broadcasting media

There are several channels for sound radio in all the Nordic countries, each channel having its own distinct character: light entertainment, education, home service, etc.

There is more than one television channel in Finland and Sweden. Of special interest is the situation in Sweden, where the two television channels are presumed to be equivalent alternatives engaged in 'stimulating rivalry'. The express object of this system was to create, within the monopoly framework, a 'pluralism' in the programme output, not least in regard to the news service.

However, experience has shown that the different news evaluation of the editorial television offices is more or less indistinguishable and that the presentation of different news items is also similar. An analysis of the news emanating from both channels over a thirty-day period discloses that only in seven cases did they differ in respect of the basic evaluation of the hundreds of news items broadcast during the period. This would appear to be mainly due to the tendency of news-evaluation standards to become highly uniform (especially since the editorial offices are required to strive for 'impartiality'), as well as to the fact that the channels are vying for the same viewers.

At first some distinct differences were observable between the programme output of the two television channels (TV2 focused more on informative programmes), but these differences have gradually become blurred. After nearly three years of experimentation with this system of 'stimulating rivalry', it seems evident that the effect has been the same as in commercially competing television companies: both channels focus on entertainment, and leave the viewers little choice.

These experiences apply also to the circumstances of the daily press. There is nothing unexpected in itself in the fact that two competing channels on the one hand back programmes with popular appeal and, on the other tend to resemble one another, since they vie for the same viewers. But this observation (which finds support from certain research studies dealing with the content of competing newspapers) constitutes a serious objection to the mass-media doctrine according to which competition favours diversity and freedom of choice.

7.4 A new grip?

It is a cardinal precept of democratic ideology to have the mass media, in interaction with their public, provide many-sided information and mould opinion independently of the government.

At the same time it is obvious that the opportunities of so doing are becoming more and more restricted.

The financial concentration of newspapers constitutes a patent threat to diversity of opinion. In addition, the remaining monopoly papers are known from experience and available research findings to adapt to their monopoly by glossing over the editorial profile, by turning into 'community papers', to borrow an American term.

The growing parliamentary pressure put on the broadcasting media has had a similar effect. The Swedish experiment of 'stimulating rivalry' between two television channels has not provided any solution.

The only counteracting factor is the growing interest in specialized publications. However, these can do no more than exert an indirect influence on mass communication itself (with the mass media editorial staffs acting as middlemen). Furthermore these publications reach only the already enlightened or convinced.

So far the solution tried has involved various attempts to keep newspaper competition alive, but if the Swedish experience is any guide, such efforts cannot amount to anything more than a rearguard action. The sums required to maintain the *status quo* are already considerable; given the dynamism inherent in competition, the amounts must be constantly increased, and soon the limit will have been reached to what the national economy can bear.

Under these circumstances probably the best way out is to help the besieged newspapers to establish a market similar to that of the periodicals.

Daily dissemination of news and commentary would then be handed over to monopoly media, daily papers and broadcasting media. Owing to factors that have already been touched upon (conformity in the news evaluation, the trend towards 'community papers', the requirement of 'impartiality' in broadcasting), it is likely that the picture of current events would become essentially identical in the different media.

It is perhaps relevant to ask now: what strategy should society select to foster the necessary diversity?

The current situation strongly recalls the time when monopoly status was accorded to one corporation in broadcasting. At that time technical reasons (the scarcity of wavelengths) argued for vesting exclusive broadcasting right in one corporation. Today, economic development has led to similar monopoly situations. Since the use of economic measures to reverse the concentration process appears to be beyond the means of the body politic, a case can be argued for investigating whether the experiences of monopoly control over broadcasting can offer any guidance for governmental regulation of other mass media as well.

A survey of different broadcasting ideologies has been made by Lindblad in a book called *Etermediernas Värld* (Malmö, 1970, fig. 18, p. 255).

The following ideologies are of special interest in Lindblad's survey:

The 'idealistic', which seeks to make the public more knowledgeable and intellectually enriched, and which assumes that popular educators and cultural workers will hold management responsibility.

The 'group-oriented', which looks after the interests of established groups and strives to give a positive picture of the society as it is.

The 'professional', which seeks to cater for all public wishes and media development, and which assumes that determining management influence is exercised by experts.

Lindblad points out that the Western world long adhered in broadcasting to the idealistic variant of the public service ideology (which Lindblad calls 'in the public's service'). However, this popular education attitude became increasingly untenable. As matters now stand, the struggle is between the group-oriented and the professional ideology.

Basically this means that exponents of established group interests are trying to influence programme policy so as to favour the *status quo*, whereas the managements of broadcasting companies are trying to safeguard a professional independence which permits a diversified output, an output that also contains elements of social criticism.

As concerns the broadcasting media, the ideologies of absolute freedom and business efficiency carried over from the press world are scarcely relevant any longer to the Nordic countries.

Nor can these selfsame ideologies be relevant to the newspapers. Developments have long ago left behind the absolute-freedom ideology; when we have to anticipate a monopolistic situation throughout it is unreasonable to say that newspapers offer the individual reader separate alternatives in the debate. The business-efficiency ideology will presumably become increasingly marked within the daily press. However, the important question is whether the community can accept this; it has the same consequences for newspaper contents that the 'group-oriented' ideology has for broadcasting, i.e. the content is shaped so as to favour the *status quo*. Otherwise it would seem to be impossible to gain the 'maximum satisfied audience'.

In the interest of the community at large, it should be considered imperative to arrange that the mass media can be harnessed in the service of change. Of the mass-media ideologies that have so far been tried out, the only one that seems to allow sufficient scope for such an undertaking at present is the professional ideology.

However, the broadcasting media have already found it hard to carry this ideology into practice and if it were applied to the daily press, it is likely that even greater difficulties would be encountered.

7.5 Some problems

The application of the professional ideology is impeded by the forms governing the ownership of the mass media.

Naturally, this also applies to the broadcasting firms. According to the ideology, the programme producer should be independent of the government and of financial interests. Actually, the government appoints the majority of members of the board of Sveriges Radio; the remaining directorships are filled by the shareholders: the popular movements, the business community and the press. The management of Sveriges Radio being cast in this mould is bound to raise major obstacles to applying the professional ideology. The board's membership in fact corresponds to the tenets underlying the group-oriented ideology.

Among the daily press firms a number do meet the demands of the professional ideology, both foundation-owned or owned by families devoted exclusively to newspaper publishing. These firms are detached from government and from financial interests other than those inherent in newspaper publishing itself.

However, a great many dailies are owned, in whole or in part, by political parties or allied organizations. Here the ownership form *per se* is a hindrance to upholding the professional ideology.

Naturally, it would be possible to change the ownership of Sveriges Radio and certain dailies in order to facilitate application of the professional ideology, but it is an open question whether the established interests, having once entrenched themselves in the mass media, can be persuaded to relinquish their ground.

The professional ideology also prescribes that the management should be in the hands of specialists. This is justified on the grounds that publicity should not be motivated by group interests or commercial considerations, but by the accountability to the public which may be ascribed to specialists. But this is to materialize over and above an elevation of the professional level, which is a slow process; it is necessary to have legislation or other rules which really assure the specialists a decisive influence over the editorial content. However, unless technical and psychological difficulties are taken into account, the enactment of legislation will run up against a snag: it must be designed so as not to interfere with a financially healthy operation of the firms.

It is difficult to envisage the transfer of responsibilities for mass communication to specialists without some form of public supervision.

In the case of Sveriges Radio, the principal instrument for this purpose has been the government-appointed Radio Council, which reviews programmes after they have been broadcast. In this examination process a dominant role has been accorded to the problem of balancing different programming interests. Thus here again, the group-oriented ideology has found support.

Therefore, should not preference be given perhaps to embodying the requisite rules in statutory law and turning over entire supervision to the courts. In a society of our kind the courts would appear to be the only authority that can be expected to be relatively unsusceptible to various group interests.

Past experience of broadcasting monopoly suggests that the formulation of rules poses formidable problems indeed. To bring about a diversified output it will probably be necessary to create guarantees over and above a statutory right of reply in order to enable the general public to gain a hearing through the mass media. On the other hand, one should not go so far as to demand impartiality or universality from every mass medium; such a stipulation actually amounts to a concession to the group-oriented ideology.

No special stimulus may be needed to bring about an independent critical examination. But the stipulation of certain quality criteria in the examination may be considered. Since every discussion of social conditions, however, implies an indivisible compound of facts and value judgements, the task will be extremely arduous. In the end, one may have to make do with the protection against libel afforded by the present Freedom of the Press Act and otherwise rely on the rising professional standard.

7.6 Summary

In a situation where it takes 110 million kronor to uphold some form of competition between newspapers of similar ambitions, it must be asked whether the community ought not to explore new avenues in order to maintain a diversified moulding of opinion.

From this two implications follow: first, the importance of supporting the efforts of financially ailing dailies to survive in other forms (for example, as weeklies); and second, of regulating monopolies which exist and are bound to arise in the daily press as a result of the professional public-service ideology which the broadcasting corporations are adopting.

At the same time, however, the elements of group orientation in both broadcasting and the printed media must be eliminated. If the avowed aims of the mass media are to satisfy the wishes of the public, to promote their own development, to offer a many-sided output and to ensure independent critical examination in interaction with the public, then the established interests in the community cannot be permitted to wield a dominant influence over mass communication.

Appendix

Socio-economic background tables

Section A: POPULATION

Population, 1900–70 (millions)

	Men	Women	Total
1900	2.5	2.6	5.1
1920	2.9	3.0	5.9
1930	3.0	3.1	6.1
1940	3.2	3.2	6.4
1950	3.5	3.5	7.0
1960	3.7	3.8	7.5
1970	4.0	4.1	8.1

Age groups of population (thousands), 1965 and 1970

Age	1965	1970	Men (1970)	Women (1970)
0–6	772	824	423	401
7–17	1,212	1,183	607	576
18–66	4,949	5,129	2,590	2,539
67+	839	945	416	529
TOTAL	7,772	8,081	4,036	4,045

Section B: ECONOMY

Gross National Product (GNP)

GNP at factor cost (1968) (million kronor):   115,600
GNP at market prices (1971) (in U.S.$ (million)):   35,680

GNP average—percentage increase

	1960–65	1965–70
Sweden	5.4	3.9
Western Europe	4.8	4.4

Percentage distribution of GNP

Private consumption: 55
Public consumption: 22
Gross investment: 24

Section C: JOURNALISTS

Social economic categories in 1969 (percentages)

	Upper	Middle	Low
Journalists	28	50	22
Swedish population	5	45	50

Educational background of Swedish journalists

	Men (%)	Women (%)
University diploma	8	12
Abiture	27	44
Lower than *abiture*	65	44

Swedish journalists' monthly salary in 1969 (kronor)

	Men (%)	Women (%)
Under 2,000	7	20
2,001–2,500	20	19
2,501–3,000	22	24
3,001–3,500	14	6
3,501–4,000	13	6
4,001–5,000	11	10
5,001+	6	1
Not known	7	14
	100	100

Section D: NEWSPAPERS

Number of towns issuing one or more daily newspapers, 1950–70

Number of dailies	1950	1960	1970
5	2	1	1[1]
4	3	2	1[2]
3	15	6	1[3]
2	31	23	17[4]
1	42	56	62

1. Stockholm.
2. Malmö.
3. Gothenburg.
4. Borås, Eskilstuna, Falun, Gävle, Jönköping, Kalmar, Karlskrona, Karlstad, Luleå, Norrköping, Skövde, Sundsvall, Umeå, Visby, Växjö, Örebro, Ostersund.

Daily newspaper sales: number of copies per 1,000 inhabitants

Year	Street sale	Subscription	Total
1945	45	386	431
1950	70	420	490
1955	84	421	505
1960	90	412	502
1965	113	419	532
1970	160	401	561

Newspapers' political tendencies, 1945 and 1970

	1945	1970	Election results
Conservatives	22.4	23.2	11.5
Folk Party	50.6	48.4	16.2
Social Democrats	14.8	21.0	45.4
Centre Party	4.8	3.0	19.9
Others	7.4	4.4	7.0

Daily-newspaper readers according to their age, education, civil status and income in 1967

		Newspaper readers (%)
	Men	97.1
	Women	95.1
Age 15–24		92.3
25–44		96.7
45–64		97.7
65–80		96.8

73

Education	Primary school	96.7
	Ten years' education	93.7
	Fifteen years' education	95.9
	Abiture	95.6
	University	100.0
Civil status	Married	97.9
	Widowed	94.9
	Divorced	100.0
	Single	92.2
Yearly income (kronor)	Under 10,000	93.2
	10,000–19,000	96.6
	20,000–39,000	97.2
	40,000–59,000	98.6
	60,000+	98.5

Consumption of evening newspapers, 1931–70 (millions of copies)

1931	1940	1950	1960	1970
81	117	206	255	323

Section E: BOOK PRODUCTION

Book production, 1965 and 1970

	1965	1970
Books and booklets	6,666	7,709
Yearbooks	708	754
Miscellaneous	26	18
Total book production	7,400	8,481

Section F: CINEMA

Number of cinemas, 1950–70

1950	1955	1960	1965	1970
2,549	2,501	2,403	1,996	1,483

Cinema spectators (millions) and origin of films shown in Sweden, 1960–70

Year	Number of spectators	Foreign productions	Swedish productions
1960	55.0	301	20
1962	50.0	301	16
1964	40.0	254	20
1966	37.3	227	23
1968	32.6	317	30
1970	28.2	253	17

Section G: RADIO AND TELEVISION

Radio and television receivers, 1963 and 1972

	Number		Receivers per 100 people	
Year	Radio	Television	Radio	Television
1963	2,844,600	1,640,000	38	22
1972	2,961,550	2,619,140	37	31.2

Duration of radio broadcasts (hours)

	1962–63	1970–71
Programme 1	7,920	5,892
Programme 2	6,116	3,069
Programme 3	1,407	8,719
TOTAL	15,443	17,680

Duration (in broadcasting hours) of national and regional radio programmes

	1968–69	1969–70
National programme	16,632	17,148
Regional programme	3,044	2,989
TOTAL	19,676	20,137

Radio and television school programmes (hours)

	1964–65	1965–66	1966–67	1967–68	1968–69	1969–70
Radio	397	442	444	418	400	405
Television	140	145	241	241	274	345

Radio-programme structure (percentages)

	Programme 1	Programme 2	Programme 3
News and current affairs	21.4	2.0	3.7
Politics and culture	24.7	0.2	0.4
Talks	12.0	31.9	
Classical music	15.8	62.0	
Light music, including jazz	8.0	2.0	82.7
Other entertainments	5.4	0.3	7.8
Miscellaneous	12.7	1.6	5.4

Duration of television programmes (hours)

1962–63	1964–65	1966–67	1968–69	1969–70
1,840	2,065	2,176	2,441	3,815

Television-programme structure, 1968–69

	Hours	%
Talks and information		
News	299	12.8
Culture	456	19.6
Religion	60	2.6
Theatre and music	198	8.5
Documentaries	49	2.1
TOTAL	1,062	45.6
Films		
Feature films	163	6.6
Television serials	214	9.2
Short films	307	13.2
TOTAL	674	29.0
Others		
Children's and youth programmes	232	10.0
Sport and leisure time	358	15.4
TOTAL	590	25.4